Strategically Establishing New Churches

Geary Reid

All Scripture quotations are from the King James Version unless otherwise noted.

ISBN: 978-976-8305-74-9.

Acknowledgments

Great thanks must be expressed to the following people:

The heavenly Father, for granting me the wisdom and inspiration to record the information in this book, which I began on December 15, 2021, and completed on December 21, 2021; my family, for their continued encouragement and support regarding various challenges; and several people who have assisted with reviewing and editing the book:

- Wonnetta Nicholson, Dipl. in Business Management and Administration
- Rev. Rickford Fanfair
- John A.S. Clowes, MSc., BSc., Dipl.
- Lincoln Robinson, Int. Dipl. In Leadership and Management, Cert. in Language and Communication

To you, the reader: have fun while reading, and grasp and practice what you learn so that this world will become a better place. Many people are depending on your guidance. We all need a shoulder to lean on and a hand to guide us.

Rev. Geary Reid

MBA, FCCA, FAAPM, MPM, CA

Reid's Learning Institute and Business Consultancy

reidnlearn.com

Amazon: amazon.com/author/gearyreid

Facebook: Reid n Learn

Instagram: Reid n Learn

LinkedIn: Reid's Learning Institute
and Business Consultancy

199 Kuru - Kururu, Soesdyke Linden Highway
Guyana, South America

Table of Contents

Introduction

The establishment of new churches must be part of the church's strategy. God wants his children to plan, and their planning must go beyond tomorrow. He wants them to prepare to reach the lost, win new souls, and retain those members. The Lord has not asked believers to do something impossible. It can become a reality if leaders organize with their congregations to plant churches.

Strategically establishing a new church requires the congregation to pray about this project. Then, as believers pray and God gives them directions, the Lord will assist them with the finances needed to start and finish the building.

There are many costs associated with the establishment of new churches. Some of these costs are fixed prices, and others are variable costs. To acquire land for the church, leaders must seek lands that are free from disputes. Acquiring commercial lands may allow leaders to attract more persons to the church. Leaders must not share the church's vision with everyone, since some persons may hate or envy them for establishing a new church. When constructing new churches, quality materials must be used. Skilled employees must also be involved in building God's house.

The strategy to establish new churches will be multifaceted, involving many persons from the congregation. Since no church leader has all the information to start and complete a new church, a steering committee will be required. The assistance of external persons may also be required—for example, project managers, lawyers, realtors, bankers, engineers, etc. In many large churches, some of the congregants may be qualified and experienced in these areas, and the church leaders must utilize the technical skills of their qualified members.

God wants his children to be in an established place. In the beginning, God met with Adam and Eve in the garden of Eden. Later, he commanded Moses to build a tabernacle to meet his people. King Solomon built a temple unto the Lord. Jesus Christ told Peter, "Upon this rock, I will build my church." Therefore, we see that God wants his people to be assembled where he can meet them regularly and give them instructions through their leaders.

Before new leaders are sent to lead new churches, they must be trained. These new leaders will need other support persons to work with them. Each church leader must possess certain qualities so that people will respect them, listen to them, and follow their ministries. The lifestyle of leaders must be good testimonies for the kingdom of God.

A great farewell service must be planned by those members assigned to the new church. For the opening ceremony of the new church, many dignitaries must be invited. Leaders must expect the presence of God to be at the opening ceremony and all other services.

1. The Great Commission

When Jesus walked on this earth doing his Father's works, he always encouraged people to know the Father. Jesus always spoke well of his Father and stated that he was doing the works of his Father.

Indeed, the Father wants people to be saved. Therefore, those who are lost need salvation, which is only available through Jesus.

After Jesus was crucified and rose again, he met with a number of persons. Before he departed, he gave the Great Commission to believers. He is expecting that every believer will continue the works that he started. Jesus wants believers to preach about the kingdom of God and encourage persons to give their lives to the Lord.

There are many souls to be saved, and believers must be prepared to go to sinners and tell them about the Lord, and specifically about the love of God. If a sinner rejects hearing God's word, believers must not be discouraged, since these sinners are rejecting the Lord and not the believers.

Salvation is a choice, and God will never force himself on anyone. If some choose not to believe, then they have condemned themselves because of that choice. You can't force anyone to be saved, scare anyone into being saved, or argue anyone into being saved.

> **John 3:18**
>
> 18 He that believeth on him is not condemned: but he that believeth not is condemned already, because he hath not believed in the name of the only begotten Son of God.

1.1 Jesus died for sinners

The Lord knew that everyone had sinned, yet he was willing to die for their sins. Jesus always wants to reconcile man unto God, so he was ready to lay down his life for sinners to have a new life in God.

Romans 5:6-12

6 For when we were yet without strength, in due time Christ
died for the ungodly. 7 For scarcely for a righteous man will one
die: yet peradventure for a good man some would even dare to
die. 8 But God commendeth his love toward us, in that, while
we were yet sinners, Christ died for us. 9 Much more then,
being now justified by his blood, we shall be saved from wrath
through him. 10 For if, when we were enemies, we were
reconciled to God by the death of his Son, much more, being
reconciled, we shall be saved by his life. 11 And not only so, but
we also joy in God through our Lord Jesus Christ, by whom
we have now received the atonement. 12 Wherefore, as by one
man sin entered into the world, and death by sin; and so death
passed upon all men, for that all have sinned.

Everyone has sinned and fallen short of God's glory; therefore, as sinners, we are in need of a Savior to save us. We were born into the Adamic sin, and our sin caused a separation from God. Christ dying for sinners brought about reconciliation, and our broken relationship was permanently fixed.

Since we are all sinners, we can all be saved. The message of salvation is a demonstration of God's unconditional love toward us. Christ dying for sinners shows us that God loves us very much, even when we were sinners. God's love doesn't change, and he loves everyone the same, from the worst of sinners to the best of believers.

1.2 Go to sinners

Since Jesus was willing to die for sinners, believers have a responsibility to go where sinners are and share the Good News. Too many believers become comfortable in God's sanctuary and do not go to the sinners.

They must remember that Jesus gave the Great Commission to all believers.

Matthew 28:18-20

18 And Jesus came and spake unto them, saying, All power is
given unto me in heaven and in earth. 19 Go ye therefore, and
teach all nations, baptizing them in the name of the Father, and
of the Son, and of the Holy Ghost: 20 Teaching them to observe
all things whatsoever I have commanded you: and, lo, I am
with you always, even unto the end of the world. Amen.

Table 1. Unfolding the Great Commission (Matthew 28:19-20)

Instruction from Jesus	Explanation
Go ye	Jesus wants every believer to know that they have an instruction from him to go and meet sinners wherever sinners are. This therefore means that the Great Commission is given to all believers and not just to the leaders of the congregation. While Jesus spoke to the disciples at that time, his message is applicable to all believers.
Teach	Sinners need to hear the truth. Therefore, believers must be prepared and willing to teach the truth. No believer must hide the truth from those who need to hear it. In sharing the word of God, teaching requires more time and effort when compared to singing. Sinners and new converts need clarity, and they need believers who will spend time sharing God's truth with them in a simple manner. The reason some sinners have not given much attention to following Christ is that many believers are not willing to go to them and teach them about God's word. The church must be a

	place that provides quality information to everyone. The church must be a house where God's word is taught, and then believers take God's word with them to the sinners (Romans 10:12-15).
All nations	There is no restriction on going different places to meet sinners (Luke 10:1-3). Believers have a borderless geographical span to reach people wherever they are. Even if some believers cannot fluently speak the native language of a group of persons, that must not stop them from sharing God's word, since they can use interpreters to translate the message.
Baptizing them in the name of the Father, and of the Son, and of the Holy Ghost	Besides teaching the sinners about God's word, believers must go the extra steps of helping sinners to understand God's word and encouraging them to be baptized. A person who wants to be baptized must be committed to following the Lord all the way. Therefore, believers must spend time with sinners, convincing them of the importance of accepting Jesus into their lives and of making a public statement through water baptism that they will follow the Lord. No believer must try to baptize sinners in their own name or the name of their church. God will only accept baptism that is done through the Father, the Son, and the Holy Ghost.
Teaching them to observe all things whatsoever I have	Teaching must be provided to the unsaved person. The unsaved person must be able to attend a place where they will be taught the word of God. This therefore means that believers must

commanded you	make a deliberate effort to teach sinners and new converts. The teaching to be provided to sinners and new converts is not one-off instruction (2 Timothy 4:2). The teaching must encourage them to follow the things of God, even when they do not feel like doing so.
I am with you always, even unto the end of the world	As believers go out to share the Good News, they must have confidence that the Lord is with them, which means that no believer is alone. So, believers must be willing to leave the sanctuary and go after sinners, then bring them back into the sanctuary to learn more of God's word (Mark 16:15-18).

When believers do their work by meeting sinners and teaching them about God's word, the sanctuary will soon be filled. Therefore, more sanctuaries will have to be constructed for sinners. New converts will need to hear God's word to establish where their spiritual life will be fed.

We must note that according to the Great Commission, we are called to make disciples of all nations. Evangelizing shouldn't just be about getting people to know the Lord, but also about discipleship. Our evangelism should be rebranded to *discipleship evangelism.*

In that way, we will make sure that we study with them, helping them grow into the Lord and understand the elementary principles of our faith. When we have one disciple, they will go and disciple another. This will eliminate "baby Christians" and produce mature believers who will be able to equip others.

2 Timothy 2:2 (NKJV)

2 And the things that you have heard from me among many witnesses, commit these to faithful men who will be able to teach others also.

The life of a believer is always active. Each believer has works to do, and God will reward them when they do his works.

1.3 Constantly sharing God's word

The word of the Lord must be preached at all times. It applies to all people and for all seasons.

> **2 Timothy 4:1-6**
>
> [1] I charge thee therefore before God, and the Lord Jesus Christ,
> who shall judge the quick and the dead at his appearing and his
> kingdom; [2] Preach the word; be instant in season, out of
> season; reprove, rebuke, exhort with all long suffering and
> doctrine. [3] For the time will come when they will not endure
> sound doctrine; but after their own lusts shall they heap to
> themselves teachers, having itching ears; [4] And they shall turn
> away their ears from the truth, and shall be turned unto fables.
> [5] But watch thou in all things, endure afflictions, do the work
> of an evangelist, make full proof of thy ministry. [6] For I am
> now ready to be offered, and the time of my departure is at
> hand.

1.4 More souls are needed for the kingdom and God's house

Jesus wants every believer to be on a mission to win more souls. There is always space in the kingdom for every soul.

Figure 1. Go teach sinners and bring them to Christ

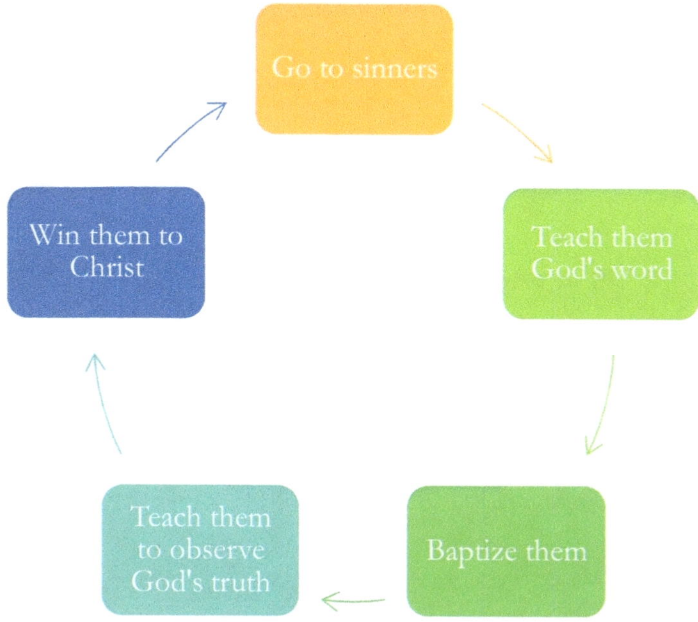

(All figures developed by the author unless otherwise noted.)

Proverbs 11:30

30 The fruit of the righteous is a tree of life; and he that winneth souls is wise.

Persons who are going to establish churches must also work on having more souls attending the house of God. The establishment of a sanctuary will allow more persons to find a fixed place to hear and receive from God. Therefore, believers must continue the Great Commission and win more souls. If that sanctuary becomes filled, then more sanctuaries must be established.

Figure 1.6 Reach sinners and bring them to Christ

2. The church's mission

Where do leaders want to see the church a decade from now? Do they plan to plant new churches? Are the current leaders of the church planning to develop new leaders? Do the current leaders embrace the understanding that the congregation that they are leading must fulfill the Great Commission?

These are some important questions that the current leaders of a church need to ask themselves. Unfortunately, some church leaders are satisfied with where they are, and they do not plan to expand their reach to other communities and people.

All believers were given the Great Commission as God's requirement for them. Therefore, church leaders must develop the church's strategy with a focus on fulfilling the Great Commission.

Church leaders may wonder what a strategic plan is. Here is an explanation of a strategic plan from a corporate viewpoint: "A company's strategic plan lays out its business purpose, future direction, performance targets and strategy" (Thompson et al., 2014).

Just as organizations strategies, churches must also develop strategies. The people of God must constantly be thinking and planning for the future. While believers are expecting Jesus Christ to return soon, they must still plan for the future until he comes.

Reaching lost souls cannot be done by default. It must be through deliberate effort. Effectively reaching sinners requires a strategy.

"A company's strategy is its action plan for outperforming its competitors and achieving superior profitability. Strategy is about competing differently from rivals – doing what competitors don't do, or, even better, doing what they can't do." (Thompson et al., 2014)

Believers must remember that they are not competing against other believers. They must plan to win their battles against Satan.

2.1 Establishing a mission statement

In some communities, there are multiple churches. However, it is important that each church have a mission statement that is known to their members. When the members know of the church's mission statement, then they may be more inclined to assist the church in fulfilling its mission.

"Mission denotes values, the business's rationale for existing; vision refers to where the organization intends to be in a few years time" (ACCA P5, 2010, p. 9).

Along with the mission statement, the church leaders should establish a plan for the church. Each year, they must plan to accomplish some important things. It will take them some time to develop their mission statement and church plan, but they must set aside the time needed to prepare these important documents. The church plan must be synchronized with the church's mission statement.

Table 2. An example of a church mission statement, five-year plan, and annual plan

Mission statement	Equipping each member to reach the lost souls by befriending them and sharing the message of Jesus Christ in X country.
Annual theme for year 1	Acquisition of assets (fundraisers and acquisition of land and properties to plant the new churches)
Annual theme for year 2	Educating and equipping the members (saints)
Annual theme for year 3	Acquiring mass communication equipment

Annual theme for year 4	Mass communication of the gospel (training persons for radio and television ministry)
Annual theme for year 5	Instituting outreaches (at the recently acquired land and properties or within the projected locations)

2.2 Annual plan for the church

Believers need to know that an annual plan is important for the church. The mission statement is often brief and will not provide information on how the church will execute its mission. However, the annual plan will give some guidance and directions on how the church will work toward fulfilling its mission each year. The church's plan must be reviewed and updated annually. If some of the activities were not completed, then those unfinished activities can be included in the annual plan for the next year if they will be taking the church in the same direction.

Figure 2. Why do you need an annual plan for a church program?

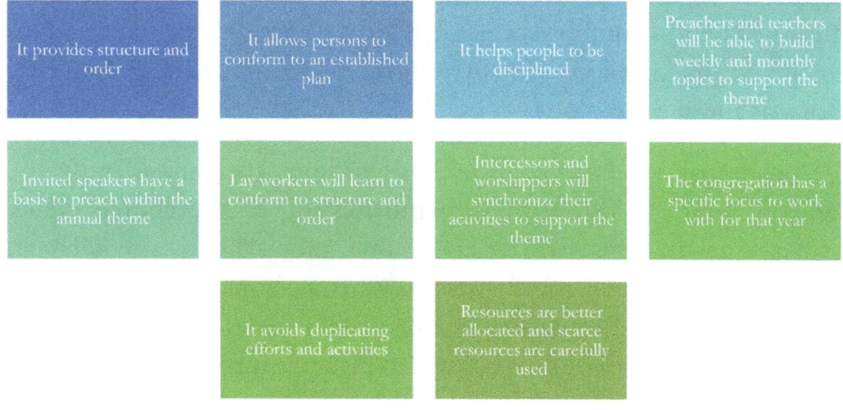

The Word of God reminds believers that "he that winneth souls is wise" (Proverbs 11:30). But winning souls must be done according to a strategy. Sinners will rarely walk into the church and seek to be saved. Therefore, believers must constantly have strategies to win souls. When new churches are established, it allows believers to reach more persons wherever they are. When persons constantly hear God's word, along with the conviction of the Holy Spirit, they will give their hearts to the Lord.

The church is one of the most influential organizations in any society, but in order for the church to be effective, believers must be active and execute the assignment given to them by God.

Planning is not a harmful thing for believers to do. King Solomon challenged believers to learn from the ant and to plan.

> **Proverbs 6:6-11**
>
> [6] Go to the ant, thou sluggard; consider her ways, and be wise:
> [7] Which having no guide, overseer, or ruler, [8] Provideth her
> meat in the summer, and gathereth her food in the harvest.
> [9] How long wilt thou sleep, O sluggard? When wilt thou arise
> out of thy sleep? [10] Yet a little sleep, a little slumber, a little
> folding of the hands to sleep: [11] So shall thy poverty come as
> one that travelleth, and thy want as an armed man.

2.3 A name for each church

Each church or house of worship must have a name, and the name must not be too complex. A name helps a church to register as a Not for Profit organization. This may allow the church to seek financing from financial institutions.

The name of the church also allows persons to easily identify the building, and it must fit in with the mission of the church. Many professional persons like to know that they will be attending an established house of God to worship. When persons in the community are impressed by the structure, organization, and efficiency of the church, they are more likely to want to be a part of it.

3. Assemble the people together

Oftentimes, God calls for his people to be assembled together in one place. When they assemble together in one place, he tells them the same information all at once.

3.1 God asked for a tabernacle to be established

There are often discussions among believers about whether there is a need to have a church at all, since everyone can worship God wherever they are. Indeed, God is a spirit and can be worshipped anywhere. However, in Exodus 25, he asked for his children to bring offerings to him, and he wanted them to bring them to the tabernacle. God was specific in his request, and he gave the details of how the first tabernacle would be established.

> **Exodus 25:1-8**
>
> 1 And the LORD spake unto Moses, saying, 2 Speak unto the
> children of Israel, that they bring me an offering: of every man
> that giveth it willingly with his heart ye shall take my offering.
> 3 And this is the offering which ye shall take of them; gold, and
> silver, and brass, 4 And blue, and purple, and scarlet, and fine
> linen, and goats' hair, 5 And rams' skins dyed red, and badgers'
> skins, and shittim wood, 6 Oil for the light, spices for anointing
> oil, and for sweet incense, 7 Onyx stones, and stones to be set
> in the ephod, and in the breastplate. 8 And let them make me a
> sanctuary; that I may dwell among them.

Further details of the tabernacle and its contents and dimension are found in Exodus chapters 25-27 and 33-40. God is specific in what he wants his children to do in order for him to bless them.

3.2 God's tabernacle through Moses

God was willing to meet with his people (Exodus 25:8), and to do this, he worked through Moses, their leader. In Exodus 33:7-11, there is an illustration of God meeting his people in one place. This became a common practice thereafter, where God meets his people as a congregation. The modern church follows a similar pattern to the tabernacle (tent) meeting.

> **Exodus 33:7-11**
>
> 7 And Moses took the tabernacle, and pitched it without the
> camp, afar off from the camp, and called it the Tabernacle of
> the congregation. And it came to pass, that every one which
> sought the LORD went out unto the tabernacle of the
> congregation, which was without the camp. 8 And it came to
> pass, when Moses went out unto the tabernacle, that all the
> people rose up, and stood every man at his tent door, and
> looked after Moses, until he was gone into the tabernacle.
> 9 And it came to pass, as Moses entered into the tabernacle, the
> cloudy pillar descended, and stood at the door of the
> tabernacle, and the Lord talked with Moses. 10 And all the
> people saw the cloudy pillar stand at the tabernacle door: and
> all the people rose up and worshipped, every man in his tent
> door. 11 And the LORD spake unto Moses face to face, as a man
> speaketh unto his friend. And he turned again into the camp:
> but his servant Joshua, the son of Nun, a young man, departed
> not out of the tabernacle.

The tabernacle was not a permanent structure but a temporary facility for God to meet with the leader and his people. In the Old Testament, when the people of God moved to another place, they would establish another tabernacle.

3.3 King Solomon built the first temple

King Solomon wanted a permanent meeting place for God to meet with his people (1 Kings 6:1-37; 2 Chronicles 2:1-18). He was willing to establish a permanent structure rather than a temporary one. The temple that King Solomon built was larger than the tabernacle that Moses had established.

1 Kings 6:1

[1] And it came to pass in the four hundred and eightieth year after the children of Israel were come out of the land of Egypt, in the fourth year of Solomon's reign over Israel, in the month Zif, which is the second month, that he began to build the house of the LORD.

3.4 God's house must not be misused

When Jesus visited the temple, he saw persons misusing this place of worship. He was displeased with their actions, so he drove them out of the temple.

Matthew 21:12

[12] And Jesus went into the temple of God, and cast out all them that sold and bought in the temple, and overthrew the tables of the moneychangers, and the seats of them that sold doves.

3.5 Common things about God's meeting place

The Lord wants to meet and interact with his people. He does not want his people to be afraid to meet with him. In the time of the Old Testament, the children of God communicated to their Maker through their leaders. However, Jesus has given believers direct access to the Lord.

Matthew 27:51

[51] And, behold, the veil of the temple was rent in twain from the top to the bottom; and the earth did quake, and the rocks rent.

In the Old and New Testaments, the words "tabernacle," "tent," "temple," "synagogue," and "church" are used to refer to a place where God will meet his people as they assemble there to hear from him. When God gave Moses instruction to build the tabernacle, God only wanted one tabernacle, and King Solomon was instructed to build only one temple. However, today, clear guidance is given for believers to build many churches to spread the gospel to every people and every nation.

Figure 3. Common things about the tabernacle, temple, synagogue, and church

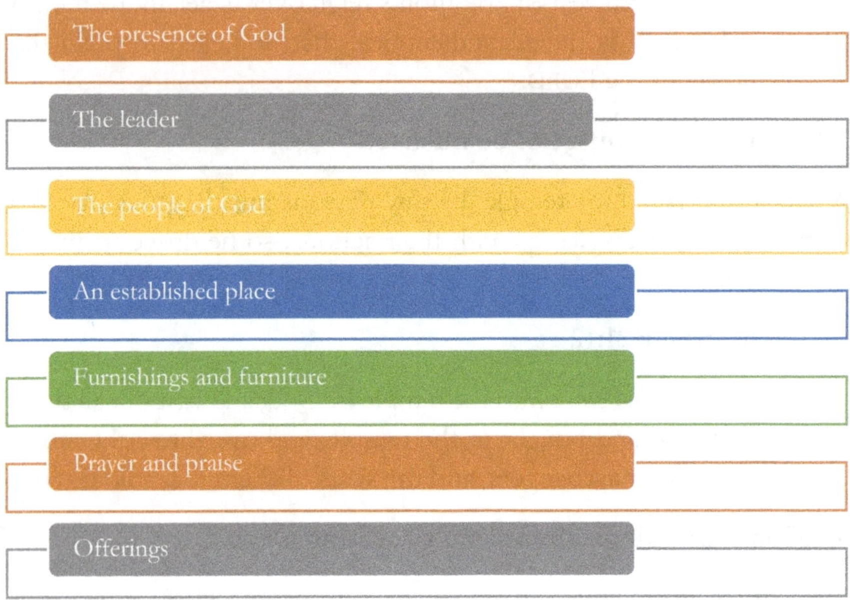

3.5.1 The presence of God

The house of worship must always include the presence of God. God loves to be among his people, so he calls for them to come and reason with him.

> **Exodus 25:22**
>
> [22] And there I will meet with thee, and I will commune with thee from above the mercy seat, from between the two cherubims which are upon the ark of the testimony, of all things which I will give thee in commandment unto the children of Israel.

3.5.2 The leader

In the house of God, the Lord often works through a leader. In the Old Testament, we see him working through men like Moses and King Solomon.

Exodus 25:1-2

[1] And the LORD spake unto Moses, saying, [2] Speak unto the children of Israel, that they bring me an offering: of every man that giveth it willingly with his heart ye shall take my offering.

2 Samuel 7:13

[13] He shall build an house for my name, and I will stablish the throne of his kingdom for ever.

When Jesus came to the earth, he gave people a new way to access the Father for themselves. No one can bypass Jesus in trying to reach the Father.

John 14:6

[6] Jesus saith unto him, I am the way, the truth, and the life: no man cometh unto the Father, but by me.

Jesus has appointed certain believers to lead the people in the presence of God. These leaders are expected to educate and inspire God's people to seek the Lord as often as possible.

Ephesians 4:11-13

[11] And he gave some, apostles; and some, prophets; and some, evangelists; and some, pastors and teachers; [12] For the perfecting of the saints, for the work of the ministry, for the edifying of the body of Christ: [13] Till we all come in the unity of the faith, and of the knowledge of the Son of God, unto a perfect man, unto the measure of the stature of the fulness of Christ.

No man is an island; therefore, leaders should not underestimate the work of the Five-Fold Ministry. Each functioning member of this ministry has a specific function, with the ultimate goal of perfecting the saints. As a result, there must be a balance in the church, and no leader should see themselves as greater than any other.

1 Corinthians 12:12 (NKJV)

12 For as the body is one and has many members, but all the members of that one body, being many, are one body, so also is Christ.

3.5.3 The people of God

God loves to interact with his people. He wants his people to come unto him.

In Isaiah 1:18, God is calling people unto himself. Many persons think that their sins will keep them away from meeting with God, but he is calling everyone, even though he knows that they have sinned.

Isaiah 1:18

18 Come now, and let us reason together, saith the LORD: though your sins be as scarlet, they shall be as white as snow; though they be red like crimson, they shall be as wool.

We must remember that the people are God's sheep, and therefore, we have a huge responsibility: to care for the sheep God has given unto us. The pulpit should be used to gather the sheep and not to scatter them. It should be used to build and not to destroy. The people of God should not feel fear when it comes to the presence of God.

1 Peter 5:2-3 (NKJV)

2 Shepherd the flock of God which is among you, serving as overseers, not by compulsion but willingly, not for dishonest
gain but eagerly; 3 nor as being lords over those entrusted to
you, but being examples to the flock.

3.5.4 An established place

God met Adam and Eve in the garden for his earliest visitation with people. However, he wants to meet his people at a specific place.

Exodus 25:8

[8] And let them make me a sanctuary; that I may dwell among them.

3.5.5 Furnishings and furniture

God commanded Moses to have some specific furnishings and furniture in the house of the Lord. King Solomon followed the example of Moses and also had these items in the house of the Lord (Exodus 25-27; 1 Kings 6). These furnishings and furniture were to be of specific dimensions and were to be arranged according to God's instructions (Exodus 25-27).

2 Chronicles 5:1

[1] Thus all the work that Solomon made for the house of the LORD was finished: and Solomon brought in all the things that David his father had dedicated; and the silver, and the gold, and all the instruments, put he among the treasures of the house of God.

3.5.6 Prayer and praise

People must enter God's presence with prayer and praise. The Lord loves to be worshipped.

2 Chronicles 5:13-14

[13] It came even to pass, as the trumpeters and singers were as one, to make one sound to be heard in praising and thanking the LORD; and when they lifted up their voice with the trumpets and cymbals and instruments of musick, and praised the LORD, saying, For he is good; for his mercy endureth for ever: that then the house was filled with a cloud, even the house of the LORD; [14] So that the priests could not stand to minister by reason of the cloud: for the glory of the LORD had filled the house of God.

Psalm 100:1-5

[1] Make a joyful noise unto the LORD, all ye lands. [2] Serve the LORD with gladness: come before his presence with singing. [3] Know ye that the LORD he is God: it is he that hath made us, and not we ourselves; we are his people, and the sheep of his pasture. [4] Enter into his gates with thanksgiving, and into his courts with praise: be thankful unto him, and bless his name. [5] For the LORD is good; his mercy is everlasting; and his truth endureth to all generations.

Jeremiah 33:3

[3] Call unto me, and I will answer thee, and show thee great and mighty things, which thou knowest not.

Our relationship with God dictates how we worship, and it for this reason that we should know the Lord for ourselves. Worship is more than singing and playing musical instruments. The Samaritan woman was told by the Lord Jesus that her people were worshipping what they did not know (John 4:22).

It is for that specific reason that we must know God. When we know God, our worship, our prayer, and even our entire persona will all be different.

3.5.7 Offerings

When God's children come into his presence, he wants them to bring something. Therefore, they must be prepared to make an offering. There are so many things that people can offer to the Lord, and this includes, but is not limited to, their very lives. God wants to forgive people for their sins.

Exodus 25:3-7

[3] And this is the offering which ye shall take of them; gold, and silver, and brass, [4] And blue, and purple, and scarlet, and fine linen, and goats' hair, [5] And rams' skins dyed red, and badgers' skins, and shittim wood, [6] Oil for the light, spices for anointing

> oil, and for sweet incense, 7 Onyx stones, and stones to be set
> in the ephod, and in the breastplate.

King Solomon worshipped God. He presented offerings to the Lord, and the Lord was pleased with Solomon's sacrifices. Those who give their best to the Lord, from a pure heart, can expect God to work on their behalf, just as he did for King Solomon.

2 Chronicles 7:1-10

> 1 Now when Solomon had made an end of praying, the fire
> came down from heaven, and consumed the burnt offering
> and the sacrifices; and the glory of the LORD filled the house.
> 2 And the priests could not enter into the house of the LORD,
> because the glory of the LORD had filled the LORD's house.
> 3 And when all the children of Israel saw how the fire came
> down, and the glory of the LORD upon the house, they bowed
> themselves with their faces to the ground upon the pavement,
> and worshipped, and praised the LORD, saying, For he is good;
> for his mercy endureth for ever. 4 Then the king and all the
> people offered sacrifices before the LORD. 5 And king
> Solomon offered a sacrifice of twenty and two thousand oxen,
> and an hundred and twenty thousand sheep: so the king and
> all the people dedicated the house of God. 6 And the priests
> waited on their offices: the Levites also with instruments of
> musick of the LORD, which David the king had made to praise
> the LORD, because his mercy endureth for ever, when David
> praised by their ministry; and the priests sounded trumpets
> before them, and all Israel stood.
>
> 7 Moreover Solomon hallowed the middle of the court that was
> before the house of the LORD: for there he offered burnt
> offerings, and the fat of the peace offerings, because the brasen
> altar which Solomon had made was not able to receive the
> burnt offerings, and the meat offerings, and the fat. 8 Also at
> the same time Solomon kept the feast seven days, and all Israel
> with him, a very great congregation, from the entering in of
> Hamath unto the river of Egypt. 9 And in the eighth day they

made a solemn assembly: for they kept the dedication of the
altar seven days, and the feast seven days. 10 And on the three
and twentieth day of the seventh month he sent the people
away into their tents, glad and merry in heart for the goodness
that the LORD had shewed unto David, and to Solomon, and
to Israel his people.

4. Be selective when sharing your vision

When God calls believers to do something great, they must know who to partner with, because they must not share their vision with everyone. Even the construction of a new church may be information to keep away from certain persons. Not everyone is always happy about what the Lord is doing in the lives of believers. It might surprise you that even your own brethren aren't in support and will try to discourage you at every opportunity.

4.1 Joseph was hated by his brethren

Within some congregations and denominations, it may be better if some visions are shared only with selected persons. After the works of the church have progressed, then others can be informed. In cases where the leaders have to seek financing from the congregation, then some information will have to be shared with them, but not all of the details.

As a young man, Joseph received dreams from God. He was excited to share his dream, and he thought it would be great to share his vision with his brethren, but it only made them hate him more. Just imagine, someone is sharing a vision with a family member, and it causes unease in the family.

Read the episode of Joseph's tragedy in Genesis 37:1-36. He chooses to tell his dreams to those he thinks will be excited to hear about them, but they want to destroy him because of his dreams. His dreams demonstrated that he would be ruler over them, and that is something they could not accept. When some pastors and leaders recognize that another pastor will be building a bigger and more modern church than theirs, it can cause them to feel envious. If some pastors and leaders know that a church is going to be built in their community, then they may be afraid that they will lose some of their members to the new church.

Genesis 37:1-36

1 And Jacob dwelt in the land wherein his father was a stranger,
in the land of Canaan. 2 These are the generations of Jacob.
Joseph, being seventeen years old, was feeding the flock with
his brethren; and the lad was with the sons of Bilhah, and with
the sons of Zilpah, his father's wives: and Joseph brought unto
his father their evil report. 3 Now Israel loved Joseph more than
all his children, because he was the son of his old age: and he
made him a coat of many colours. 4 And when his brethren saw
that their father loved him more than all his brethren, they
hated him, and could not speak peaceably unto him.

5 And Joseph dreamed a dream, and he told it his brethren: and
they hated him yet the more. 6 And he said unto them, Hear, I
pray you, this dream which I have dreamed: 7 For, behold, we
were binding sheaves in the field, and, lo, my sheaf arose, and
also stood upright; and behold, your sheaves stood round
about, and made obeisance to my sheaf. 8 And his brethren said
to him, Shalt thou indeed reign over us? Or shalt thou indeed
have dominion over us? And they hated him yet the more for
his dreams, and for his words.

9 And he dreamed yet another dream, and told it his brethren,
and said, Behold, I have dreamed a dream more; and behold,
the sun and the moon and the eleven stars made obeisance to
me. 10 And he told it to his father, and to his brethren: and his
father rebuked him, and said unto him, what is this dream that
thou hast dreamed? Shall I and thy mother and thy brethren
indeed come to bow down ourselves to thee to the earth?
11 And his brethren envied him; but his father observed the
saying.

12 And his brethren went to feed their father's flock in
Shechem. 13 And Israel said unto Joseph, do not thy brethren

feed the flock in Shechem? Come, and I will send thee unto them. And he said to him, here am I. [14] And he said to him, Go, I pray thee, see whether it be well with thy brethren, and well with the flocks; and bring me word again. So, he sent him out of the vale of Hebron, and he came to Shechem. [15] And a certain man found him, and behold, he was wandering in the field: and the man asked him, saying, What seekest thou? [16] And he said, I seek my brethren: tell me, I pray thee, where they feed their flocks. [17] And the man said, They are departed hence; for I heard them say, Let us go to Dothan. And Joseph went after his brethren and found them in Dothan.

[18] And when they saw him afar off, even before he came near unto them, they conspired against him to slay him. [19] And they said one to another, Behold, this dreamer cometh. [20] Come now therefore, and let us slay him, and cast him into some pit, and we will say, Some evil beast hath devoured him: and we shall see what will become of his dreams. [21] And Reuben heard it, and he delivered him out of their hands; and said, Let us not kill him. [22] And Reuben said unto them, Shed no blood, but cast him into this pit that is in the wilderness, and lay no hand upon him; that he might rid him out of their hands, to deliver him to his father again.

[23] And it came to pass, when Joseph was come unto his brethren, that they stript Joseph out of his coat, his coat of many colours that was on him; [24] And they took him and cast him into a pit: and the pit was empty, there was no water in it. [25] And they sat down to eat bread: and they lifted up their eyes and looked, and behold, a company of Ishmeelites came from Gilead with their camels bearing spicery and balm and myrrh, going to carry it down to Egypt. [26] And Judah said unto his brethren, What profit is it if we slay our brother, and conceal his blood? [27] Come, and let us sell him to the Ishmeelites, and let not our hand be upon him; for he is our brother and our flesh. And his brethren were content.

> 28 Then there passed by Midianites merchantmen; and they
> drew and lifted up Joseph out of the pit, and sold Joseph to the
> Ishmeelites for twenty pieces of silver: and they brought
> Joseph into Egypt. 29 And Reuben returned unto the pit; and
> behold, Joseph was not in the pit; and he rent his clothes.
> 30 And he returned unto his brethren, and said, The child is not;
> and I, whither shall I go?
>
> 31 And they took Joseph's coat, and killed a kid of the goats,
> and dipped the coat in the blood; 32 And they sent the coat of
> many colours, and they brought it to their father; and said, This
> have we found: know now whether it be thy son's coat or no.
> 33 And he knew it, and said, It is my son's coat; an evil beast
> hath devoured him; Joseph is without doubt rent in pieces.
> 34 And Jacob rent his clothes, and put sackcloth upon his loins,
> and mourned for his son many days. 35 And all his sons and all
> his daughters rose up to comfort him; but he refused to be
> comforted; and he said, For I will go down into the grave unto
> my son mourning. Thus, his father wept for him. 36 And the
> Midianites sold him into Egypt unto Potiphar, an officer of
> Pharaoh's, and captain of the guard.

The relationship between Joseph and his brethren became bitter. They gave him the nickname of "dreamer" (Genesis 37:19). Joseph did not do anything to harm their lives, but they hated him all the more because of his dream. What a tough situation for Joseph to find himself in!

Figure 4. Reasons why Joseph's brothers hated him

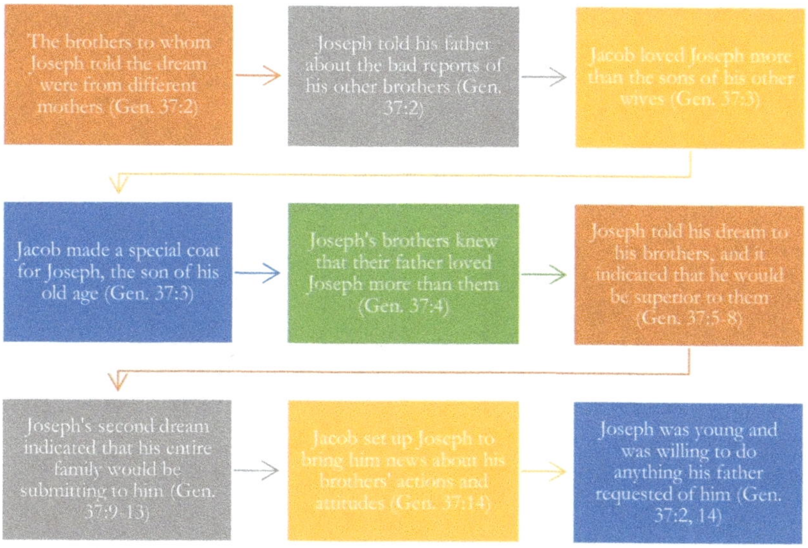

The brothers to whom Joseph told the dream were from different mothers (Gen. 37:2)

Joseph told his father about the bad reports of his other brothers (Gen. 37:2)

Jacob loved Joseph more than the sons of his other wives (Gen. 37:3)

Jacob made a special coat for Joseph, the son of his old age (Gen. 37:3)

Joseph's brothers knew that their father loved Joseph more than them (Gen. 37:4)

Joseph told his dream to his brothers, and it indicated that he would be superior to them (Gen. 37:5-8)

Joseph's second dream indicated that his entire family would be submitting to him (Gen. 37:9-13)

Jacob set up Joseph to bring him news about his brothers' actions and attitudes (Gen. 37:14)

Joseph was young and was willing to do anything his father requested of him (Gen. 37:2, 14)

There are some pastors and church leaders who are competing for church members rather than trying to win those who are lost and need the Lord. When there are several churches in the same community that are very close to each other, it can cause misunderstanding among the leaders.

It is good for church leaders to share their vision with persons who are progressing. Look for persons who have a similar burden and share the vision with them so that good feedback will be received. Also, support and wisdom might be received from leaders who have planted churches, as they will not be afraid of more churches being established.

5. Continue building

Nehemiah wanted to restore the wall that was broken down. As he was working for God, he faced much opposition. This is something that believers must become familiar with, that while they are working for God, people will say negative things about them. However, the believer must not be distracted but continue building.

Many church leaders have started to erect a building for the people of God to meet and worship the King. However, as they build, many persons may pass and see the work that they are doing, and some will use insulting words. Nevertheless, believers must adopt an approach like Nehemiah and continue the work of the Lord. If Nehemiah had paid more attention to what the naysayers were saying, the wall might not have been completed.

Building a sanctuary takes much time and money, but it is important to build it. While Nehemiah had a wall to build, believers have churches to establish. Just as Nehemiah did not give much attention to the people who thought that he could not complete the work, believers must do the same thing today.

Nehemiah 6:1-4

6 Now it came to pass when Sanballat, and Tobiah, and
Geshem the Arabian, and the rest of our enemies, heard that I
had builded the wall, and that there was no breach left therein;
(though at that time I had not set up the doors upon the gates;)
2 That Sanballat and Geshem sent unto me, saying, Come, let
us meet together in some one of the villages in the plain of
Ono. But they thought to do me mischief. 3 And I sent
messengers unto them, saying, I am doing a great work, so that
I cannot come down: why should the work cease, whilst I leave

it, and come down to you? [4] Yet they sent unto me four times
after this sort; and I answered them after the same manner.

5.1 Say no to distractors

As Nehemiah continued building the wall, his enemies sent a message requesting a meeting with him (Nehemiah 6:2). This happened on four occasions, and all four times, Nehemiah did not allow his enemies to distract him (Nehemiah 6:2-4). This speaks about a man who is focused on what he has to do and will not be distracted by his enemies.

When leaders are establishing new churches, they have to learn to say no to some invitations. Every time a leader or member moves away from whatever they are doing for the Lord, they will slow down the progress. God's people must have the motto of "Don't stop the progress" as they continue to labor in his vineyard.

Nehemiah's enemies wanted him to slow down building the wall, and if they were able to talk to him, their negative words would cause him to change his plan. Remain focused and continue building the wall!

Nehemiah was not distracted by the fifth message that he received from his enemies. He was not fearful but sent them a reply (Nehemiah 6:5-9). Take note, Nehemiah did not waste his energy by spending time having a sit-down conversation with his enemies. He was too busy building the wall to protect the people of God.

Nehemiah continued to pray that God would strengthen his hands to rebuild the wall (Nehemiah 6:9). This shows that Nehemiah was not going to get involved in ordinary fights with his enemies. He left his enemies in the hands of God.

For those leaders who are constructing a building to house God's people, be aware that there will be many distractors. However, do not allow the distractors to stop you from completing the house of the Lord.

Nehemiah 6:5-9

[5] Then sent Sanballat his servant unto me in like manner the
fifth time with an open letter in his hand; [6] Wherein was

written, It is reported among the heathen, and Gashmu saith it, that thou and the Jews think to rebel: for which cause thou buildest the wall, that thou mayest be their king, according to these words. 7 And thou hast also appointed prophets to preach of thee at Jerusalem, saying, There is a king in Judah: and now shall it be reported to the king according to these words. Come now therefore, and let us take counsel together. 8 Then I sent unto him, saying, There are no such things done as thou sayest, but thou feignest them out of thine own heart. 9 For they all made us afraid, saying, Their hands shall be weakened from the work, that it be not done. Now therefore, O God, strengthen my hands.

5.2 Do not listen to false prophets

Tobiah and Sanballat teamed up with a prophet to distract Nehemiah. However, Nehemiah was in tune with God, and he knew that they were planning to discredit him, so he did not follow the prophet Noadiah (Nehemiah 6:10-17). This shows Nehemiah to be a man who has a passion for God and who is also listening to God, even while working diligently on an important assignment for God.

Nehemiah 6:10-19

10 Afterward I came unto the house of Shemaiah the son of Delaiah the son of Mehetabeel, who was shut up; and he said, Let us meet together in the house of God, within the temple, and let us shut the doors of the temple: for they will come to slay thee; yea, in the night will they come to slay thee. 11 And I said, Should such a man as I flee? and who is there, that, being as I am, would go into the temple to save his life? I will not go in. 12 And, lo, I perceived that God had not sent him; but that he pronounced this prophecy against me: for Tobiah and Sanballat had hired him. 13 Therefore was he hired, that I should be afraid, and do so, and sin, and that they might have matter for an evil report, that they might reproach me. 14 My God, think thou upon Tobiah and Sanballat according to

> these their works, and on the prophetess Noadiah, and the rest of the prophets, that would have put me in fear.
>
> 15 So the wall was finished in the twenty and fifth day of the month Elul, in fifty and two days. 16 And it came to pass, that when all our enemies heard thereof, and all the heathen that were about us saw these things, they were much cast down in their own eyes: for they perceived that this work was wrought of our God. 17 Moreover in those days the nobles of Judah sent many letters unto Tobiah, and the letters of Tobiah came unto them. 18 For there were many in Judah sworn unto him, because he was the son in law of Shechaniah the son of Arah; and his son Johanan had taken the daughter of Meshullam the son of Berechiah. 19 Also they reported his good deeds before me, and uttered my words to him. And Tobiah sent letters to put me in fear.

Nehemiah took his complaint to God and not to the people. As a human, he could have been distracted, but he placed his faith in God. So, once God has given the approval to build his house, then go ahead and build the Lord's house.

As believers in this dispensation, we must look at everything through the lens of God's Word. God's Word takes precedence over the opinion of men. Hold on to God's Word and the Word will expose those wolves in sheep's clothing.

6. Pray for God's direction and approval

Looking to establish a new church is not an academic activity. It requires much prayer and hearing what God has to say.

Proverbs 19:21

21 There are many devices in a man's heart; nevertheless the counsel of the LORD, that shall stand.

Establishing more places of worship is something that the Lord delights in. It is God that can build the church and watch over it.

Psalm 127:1

1 Except the LORD build the house, they labour in vain that build it: except the LORD keep the city, the watchman waketh but in vain.

Jesus asked a question of his disciples, wanting to know if they really knew him. Some of them had different views about him, but Peter provided the most suitable answer.

Matthew 16:16-20

16 And Simon Peter answered and said, Thou art the Christ, the
Son of the living God. 17 And Jesus answered and said unto
him, Blessed art thou, Simon Barjona: for flesh and blood hath
not revealed it unto thee, but my Father which is in heaven.
18 And I say also unto thee, That thou art Peter, and upon this
rock I will build my church; and the gates of hell shall not
prevail against it. 19 And I will give unto thee the keys of the
kingdom of heaven: and whatsoever thou shalt bind on earth
shall be bound in heaven: and whatsoever thou shalt loose on

earth shall be loosed in heaven. [20] Then charged he his disciples
that they should tell no man that he was Jesus the Christ.

Jesus told them that he was going to build the church. This is the first time in the Bible that the word "church" was used (Matthew 16:18). Since Jesus will build his church on the truth, then believers must constantly pray.

The life of Jesus was always a life of prayer. He did not venture out into anything unless he prayed. Believers must follow this pattern from Jesus and make sure that whatever they plan to do, they undergird it with prayer. These are some things that believers can pray about when considering establishing new churches:

- God will show them possible areas for church planning
- God will send the financial resources to build the church
- The new leaders will be identified and be willing to start the new church
- There will be enough members to lead the new church in the different areas of ministry
- The purchase of land will become easy, and there will be enough space on the land for future developments
- Skilled and talented workers will be available to build the church
- Many new souls will be added to the new church
- God's presence will always be with the new congregation

These are only some of the areas to pray for when considering establishing new churches. Some church leaders will task the intercessor department with making a list such as the one above to be part of their regular prayer meetings.

God's Word reminds believers to ask for whatever they need from God. If it is according to his will, he will grant it unto them.

Matthew 7:7-8

[7] Ask, and it shall be given you; seek, and ye shall find; knock,
and it shall be opened unto you: [8] For every one that asketh

> receiveth; and he that seeketh findeth; and to him that knocketh it shall be opened.

6.1 Involvement of intercessors

Planting a new church is a strategic decision for any church leader, and it requires much prayer. God needs his children to spread his gospel with many persons, but Satan often wants to distract God's plans, as he is always jealous of God's kingdom being expanded. When intercessors are involved, they will clear those obstacles that the adversary wants to use to distract the plans of God.

Daniel spent three weeks praying, and God heard his prayer. However, the adversary withheld his prayer, and God had to send Michael, one of the chief angels, to release it.

> **Daniel 10:10-14**
>
> 10 And, behold, an hand touched me, which set me upon my
> knees and upon the palms of my hands. 11 And he said unto me,
> O Daniel, a man greatly beloved, understand the words that I
> speak unto thee, and stand upright: for unto thee am I now
> sent. And when he had spoken this word unto me, I stood
> trembling. 12 Then said he unto me, Fear not, Daniel: for from
> the first day that thou didst set thine heart to understand, and
> to chasten thyself before thy God, thy words were heard, and
> I am come for thy words. 13 But the prince of the kingdom of
> Persia withstood me one and twenty days: but, lo, Michael, one
> of the chief princes, came to help me; and I remained there
> with the kings of Persia. 14 Now I am come to make thee
> understand what shall befall thy people in the latter days: for
> yet the vision is for many days.

God's assignments for his children are no ordinary assignments. Because Satan knows that, he will try everything to prevent the will of God from being fulfilled.

Before Jesus started his earthly ministry, he spent time in prayer and fasting. He knew the importance of prayer, and he was not going to leave any room for Satan to distract the plans that God had for him.

An intercessor cannot take the place of Christ. Therefore, intercessors can't follow Moses' example and try to become a mediator. We have a mediator; therefore, our prayers are different, and intercessors should be au fait with the New Covenant.

6.2 Agreement in prayer

God wants his children to agree when they pray. Therefore, the initial plan to establish new churches must be discussed with key members of the church. Those who have information about this plan must spend time in prayer that God will make it a reality. Whenever they pray about the establishment of the new church, they must be in agreement. God is willing to answer the prayer of his children, but he wants them to be in agreement.

> **Matthew 18:18-19**
>
> 18 Verily I say unto you, Whatsoever ye shall bind on earth shall be bound in heaven: and whatsoever ye shall loose on earth shall be loosed in heaven.
> 19 Again I say unto you, That if two of you shall agree on earth as touching any thing that they shall ask, it shall be done for them of my Father which is in heaven.

6.3 Paul encouraged the believers to pray

The Apostle Paul asked the believers to pray that God would open a door for the gospel to be shared. He knew that he could not do the work of the Lord alone.

> **Colossians 4:2-3**
>
> 2 Continue in prayer, and watch in the same with thanksgiving;
> 3 Withal praying also for us, that God would open unto us a door of utterance, to speak the mystery of Christ, for which I am also in bonds.

7. Establish a steering committee

To build a church and furnish it requires the input of many persons. Sometimes church leaders need to incorporate many technical persons in this strategic decision. Establishing a new church is not like planning a kitchen garden. When a church is established, the decision-makers must conceptualize it to meet the needs of many generations. The structure that is established must be able to facilitate all the furnishings that will be added to the building. If the leaders would like to increase the size of the building in the near future, then they must factor that information into its current design. For example, if there are limited funds at the initial stage, then leaders may want to construct one flat, and then in a few years, they will add another flat to the building.

Besides the structure, there may be legal matters that the steering committee will have to address through the service of an attorney at law. For example, the purchase of land will need the opinion of a legal representative. Civil and electrical engineers will have to share their views about the new building, since there will be things that require the input of technical representatives.

The layout of the furnishings may be considered at the initial stage of the building design. Therefore, the views of interior designers will also be important.

"A steering committee is a collection of members from the various departments within the organization and is not, therefore, biased toward one particular functional area of the business" (ACCA 2.1, 2001).

The steering committee will provide wise counsel for the preparation and execution of the project. In different organizations and groups, the size and composition of a steering committee will vary. However, these are some possible persons who can be included in a church's committee for the design and building of a new church. This list is not in order of priority, and it must only be used as an example, since each church will have different needs.

- General overseer
- District overseer
- Senior pastor
- Leader who will be assigned to the new church
- Intercessors
- Financial specialist/banker
- Lawyer
- Secretary/administrator
- Civil and electrical engineer
- Project manager
- Interior decorator

7.1 Project manager

While everyone will have knowledge of what will need to be done, at least one person must have full oversight of the project. Many pastors and church leaders would like to be in charge of the project, but they must allow those who have the time and technical knowledge to manage the project.

"A project is a temporary endeavour undertaken to create a unique product, service or result. The temporary nature of projects indicates a definite beginning and end. The end is reached when the project's objectives have been achieved or when the project is terminated because its objectives will not or cannot be met, or when the need for the project no longer exists" (PMBOK 4, 2008).

The project manager must be given autonomy to manage the project from beginning to end. This person will be expected to meet with the steering committee on a regular basis to share information about the project's progress and receive feedback from the steering committee.

If it is possible, some of the meetings for the steering committee can be held very close to the worksite, or they can visit the worksite and then have their meetings. This approach will provide the committee with first-hand information for important decision-making.

"In addition to any area-specific skills and general management proficiencies required for the project, effective project management requires that the project manager possess the following characteristics" (PMBOK 4, 2008).

Table 3. Characteristics of a project manager

Characteristics	Explanation
Knowledge	This refers to what the project manager knows about project management.
Performance	This refers to what the project manager is able to do or accomplish while applying their project management knowledge.
Personal	This refers to how the project manager behaves when performing the project or related activity. Personal effectiveness encompasses attitudes, core personality characteristics and leadership–the ability to guide the project team while achieving project objectives and balancing the project constraints.

(Extracted from PMBOK 4, 2008)

7.2 Importance of the project manager

The church leaders must not appoint relatives and friends to manage the project, as the skills required for the project must come from someone who knows what has to be done. The cost of the project is too significant to be placed in the hands of a novice. The quality of work that has to be done must meet the standard established by the steering committee.

Figure 5. The church's project manager forms the link with the construction firm and key stakeholders

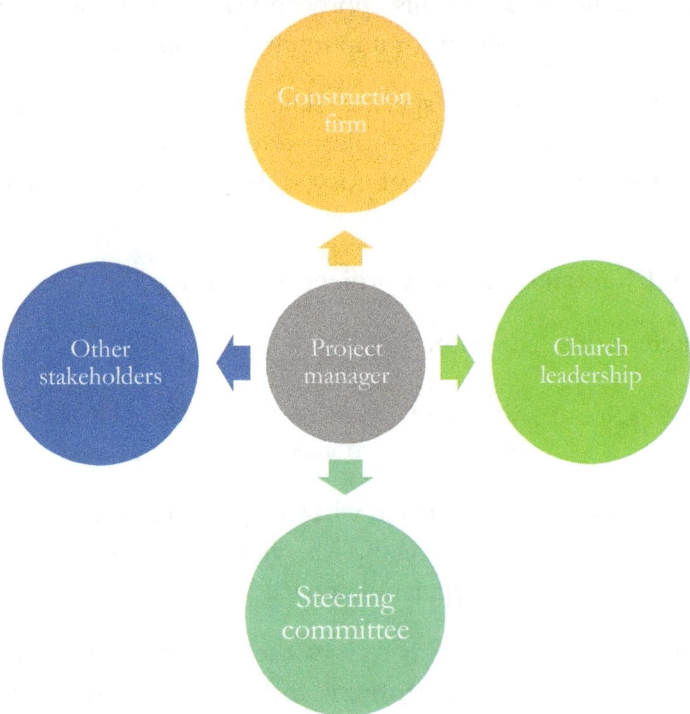

The project manager may have to be in a full-time position, in which case that person must be adequately compensated for their time and technical knowledge. When the cost of the project is prepared, it must include the compensation of the project manager.

Certain works for the Lord cannot be done for free. God often expects that his people will compensate those who use their skills to labor in his vineyard. Compensating the project manager and others who work on the project will allow them to give their best service and spend enough time on the project.

Deuteronomy 24:15

15 At his day thou shalt give him his hire, neither shall the sun go down upon it; for he is poor, and setteth his heart upon it: lest he cry against thee unto the LORD, and it be sin unto thee.

1 Corinthians 3:14

14 If any man's work abide which he hath built thereupon, he shall receive a reward.

Other members of the steering committee may be occupied with many other things and not have much time to spend supervising the project. Even if other committee members dedicate their time toward the project, they may not have the skills and knowledge of the project manager. It is important to analyze the core skills expected of most project managers.

Table 4. Core skills

Skills	Explanation
Leadership	Project managers should be able to stimulate action, progress and change.
Technological understanding	Project managers need to have an accurate perception of the technical requirements of the project so that business needs are addressed and satisfied.
Evaluation and decision-making	Project managers should have the ability to evaluate alternatives and to make informed decisions.
People management	Project managers should be able to motivate and enthuse their teams and have a constant personal drive toward achieving the project's goal.
Systems design and maintenance	Project managers should be able to demonstrate their individual competence and have complete working knowledge of the internal administration of their project.
Planning and control	Project managers should be constantly monitoring progress against the plan and taking

	any necessary corrective action using modern planning and monitoring methods.
Financial awareness	Project managers should be proficient in risk management and have a broad financial knowledge.
Procurement	Project managers should understand the basics of procurement and be able to develop the procurement strategy for the project.
Communication	Project managers should be able to express themselves clearly and unambiguously in speaking and writing and be able to do this in a wide range of situations and with a wide range of people.
Negotiation	Project managers should be skillful in managing their clients and should be able to plan and carry out a negotiation strategy
Contractual skills	Project managers should be able to understand the contract that defines their project and should be able to manage subcontractors to ensure that the contractual terms are met.
Legal awareness	Project managers should have an awareness of any legal issues that could affect their project.

(Extracted from ACCA 2.1, 2001, according to Yeates & Cadle)

From the core skills required by a project manager, it is clear that the pastor may not be the best person to manage the project. Therefore, the church leaders must allow professional persons to do their work.

8. Choose location wisely

Location is very important for the erection of a church building. Believers must see a church as a beacon of God. Many persons are happy when a church is within their community.

When there is a church in a community, it signifies the presence of God. While it must be noted that God is omnipresent and does not need a building to reside in, he is delighted to meet his people in one place at the same time.

8.1 Prime location

If the leadership of the church has to purchase land to build a church, then they must be strategic in their choice. They should not choose to purchase land that everyone has refused because they believe there are challenges with it, as the land will likely be subject to flooding and erosion.

8.2 Considerations when purchasing land for the church

Prime lands will be sold for a higher price than those lands that are not commercial lands, but the children of God must be willing to invest in this great work of the Lord. The church members may think that they do not have all the money they need to acquire the land, but they serve a God who will provide for his children when they seek him.

Figure 6. Considerations when purchasing land to build a church

- Free from disputes and title is transferable
- Strategic location
- Enough space for parking
- Enough space for future development
- Easy access to public transportation and access roads
- Low price and good location
- Zoning
- Cost for land development

8.2.1 Free from disputes and title is transferable

Church leaders must carry out enough research before signing any document to acquire land for the church, as they must make sure that the land is free from disputes. There are some lands that have been unoccupied for a long time, but that is because there are legal challenges with them. For example, there may be a dispute among family members in determining who owns the land and who has the right to sell it.

The person or organization that is engaged in the transaction to sell the land must be able to provide a title for it. They must have the power to legally sell the land.

Too often, land sales have many disputes, and churches are caught in some of those disputes. From the steering committee, the lawyer or realtor may be able to do some research to ensure that the land title is transferable.

8.2.2 Strategic location

Leaders must look for a strategic location. They are working for God, who always loves the best. They must not try to purchase land that everyone is rejecting, as the land must be strategically chosen to allow the church to have an influence in society. When organizations are looking for lands to establish their businesses, they understand the importance of location, and so they are very careful in making their choice. The children of God must follow a similar example and look for strategic locations when purchasing church lands.

8.2.3 Enough space for parking

Leaders must remember that the church is a place where many persons want to attend. However, if parking is limited or not available, then some persons will not visit the church. Many dignitaries and wealthy persons like to know that they can park their vehicles in a safe and secure place. Limited parking space may also contribute to limited attendance for church services.

8.2.4 Enough space for future development

The current church leadership does not know what will happen within the next 20 to 50 years. However, if the church land that they are about to purchase has enough space for future development, then they are making a great decision. Leaders must know that the decision they will make today must also benefit them and many other generations in the years to come. Therefore, look for land that has enough space for future development, including children's church, a business center, erection of a church college, etc.

8.2.5 Easy access to public transportation and access roads

The land must provide easy access to public and private transportation. Not all church members will own vehicles. Therefore, if they use public transportation, it must be easy for them to reach the church.

Even persons who have private transportation must not have difficulty locating the church for the first time. The location must allow for All

Wheel Drive (AWD) and four-wheel (4WD) drive vehicles to reach the church, and even vehicles that have low tires.

8.2.6 Low price and good location

The price that the land will be sold for must not be exorbitant. It must allow the church members to be able to purchase the land with ease. If the land is very expensive and the church has to seek long-term financing just to purchase it, then it may also take them many years to complete the church building.

The land must be situated in a good location. For example, many church leaders will not want to purchase land next to a dump site or noisy surroundings. The land itself must be in good condition. For example, church leaders will not want to purchase land in areas where extractive companies have extracted natural resources from the earth and the lands are uneven.

8.2.7 Zoning

In some communities, there are zoning regulations. Therefore, churches may not be allowed to be established in those communities. The zoning may also determine the size of lands that may be available for sale in that community, so if the church leaders want to erect a large building, they may be restricted from doing so.

Due to zoning, churches may have to be air-conditioned or sealed from allowing noise to emanate from the building. The buildings may also have to be similar in color, height, and size.

8.2.8 Cost for land development

Prime land may be expensive, but there will be little development work that has to be done to the land. If the development cost to level and make the land ready for construction is expensive, then the overall cost to erect a church building will also be high.

Land that has been affected by erosion and flooding may require high costs to make it ready for construction. If there were other structures on the land, then there may also be additional costs to remove them and make the land ready for construction.

8.3 Where to gather information about land for sale

Because the church leadership has the vision to establish a new church, they will have to gather information about available lands. This information will not come to them easily or in the timing they want, so they must have mechanisms in place to become aware of lands that are available.

These are some things that leaders can do to know when lands are available:

- Make it a matter of prayer and let God intervene
- Ask members of the congregation to gather information about legally available lands
- Employ the service of a realtor
- Engage with land surveyors
- Engage with land court lawyers
- Inquire about lands that banks will repossess because the clients default on their payments
- Read daily newspapers for land-related matters
- Listen to radio and television for lands that are available for sale
- Listen for government developments of new housing schemes

These are just some of the options that are available for believers to learn about lands that can be purchased for the erection of a church building. Believers cannot be idle and expect that God will do everything for them. While believers pray, they must be working and looking for opportunities to purchase a piece of land for the expansion of God's work.

It is important to read about this industrious woman in Proverbs 31. She thinks and lives business. She is constantly looking for opportunities to make great things happen, and she will not rest until she is successful. Many believers, both male and female, need to be strategists like her.

Proverbs 31:14-18

[14] She is like the merchants' ships; she bringeth her food from afar. [15] She riseth also while it is yet night, and giveth meat to her household, and a portion to her maidens. [16] She considereth a field, and buyeth it: with the fruit of her hands she planteth a vineyard. [17] She girdeth her loins with strength, and strengtheneth her arms. [18] She perceiveth that her merchandise is good: her candle goeth not out by night.

9. Project costs

Establishing a physical place for people to meet and worship the Lord has a cost attached to it. Hence, it is important to plan for this important assignment strategically.

9.1 Know the cost first

Jesus provided a good illustration when he taught about persons sitting down and counting the cost before building a tower (Luke 14:28). His example provides an understanding that cost is important and that persons must be strategic in what they want to do.

Jesus's example is applicable now, just as it was then. He asked the question of who would want to build a tower without sitting down to count the cost before moving forward. When he spoke about sitting down and counting the cost, he wanted persons to be strategic, as planning for a major event is not something that must be done in a rush. A major investment of this nature requires the investor to know what he or she wants to do and to know if the money they currently have is sufficient to take them past the foundation.

> **Luke 14:28-32**
>
> 28 For which of you, intending to build a tower, sitteth not
> down first, and counteth the cost, whether he have sufficient
> to finish it? 29 Lest haply, after he hath laid the foundation, and
> is not able to finish it, all that behold it begin to mock him,
> 30 Saying, This man began to build, and was not able to finish.
> 31 Or what king, going to make war against another king, sitteth
> not down first, and consulteth whether he be able with ten
> thousand to meet him that cometh against him with twenty
> thousand? 32 Or else, while the other is yet a great way off, he
> sendeth an ambassage, and desireth conditions of peace.

Table 5. Jesus's strategic advice for constructing a tower or going to war (Luke 14:28-32)

Major advice from Jesus	Explanation
Strategic planning	"Sitteth not down first" (v. 28). Jesus wants persons to be strategic. He asked whether persons will first sit down and plan whatever they need to do. He implies that they should not start and then sit down and plan afterward, but rather, they will sit down and plan first, and then start whatever they want to accomplish.
Financial planning	"Counteth the cost, whether he have sufficient to finish it" (v. 28). Most strategic decisions have financial implications. The costs cannot be ignored. There may be both fixed and variable costs. Without strategic planning, the cost of investment (project cost) may appear to be small, but during the time of the project, there may be cost overruns due to poor planning.
Managing public image and perception	"All that behold it begin to mock him" (v. 29). Being unable to finish any project often causes public embarrassment. Therefore, strategic planning and financial planning are important things that must be done at the beginning, since without those,

	there will be negative feedback and perception from the public.
Advisor or consultant	"Sitteth not down first, and consulteth" (v. 31). There is often the need to learn and hear from professional persons who have the know-how to start and complete any task. When seeking advice from persons, it does not mean that all the advice received will be implemented. However, it provides additional information to consider.
Team effort	"Consulteth" (v. 31). The success of many major events and projects requires team effort. Each leader must understand that he or she does not know everything. Therefore, they must seek the input of those who are more familiar with the matter of concern.

It is a waste of money to start a foundation and then not have enough money to complete the building (Luke 14:29-30). Once again, leaders who want to build a church must sit down and properly plan this major investment. This planning cannot happen during one five-minute church meeting with the leader of God's house, a few church members, and some family members.

9.2 Architecture design

Before any work starts for the construction of a sanctuary, leaders must be disciplined enough to sit down and share their views of what they need the building to look like. Leaders must pray for God's direction and blessings before they think about or start working on any church building. Building a church always requires the wisdom of God, since God knows what he wants to do through the sanctuary.

The services of a professional architect or architectural firm may have to be engaged to provide a professional drawing of the building. It is through this blueprint that the contractor will construct the building.

Sometimes, leaders must share their views of how they want to see the the building designed, and there are other times when they need to allow the technical persons to guide them about certain important adjustments. For example, a pastor may not be a civil engineer, so the pastor must know his or her limitations and allow the guidance of a professional person to give guidance. However, if the pastor is working with specific dimensions given to him or her by God, then that will be the design of the building.

Once the architectural drawing is completed and approved by the authorized persons within the church, then church leaders can display the drawing for persons to see what the sanctuary will look like. The intention of allowing persons to see the plans for the building is to get them to pray for the building to be completed soon and to give financially toward the construction of the sanctuary.

It may be costly to recruit the service of professional architects, but it is a worthwhile cost to incur. Doing the work of the Lord will always have a cost associated with it.

King David set a great example for many believers to follow. He wanted to make a sacrifice to God, and he wanted that sacrifice to cost him something. He was willing to put money behind his sacrifice.

> **2 Samuel 24:24**
>
> 24 And the king said unto Araunah, Nay; but I will surely buy it of thee at a price: neither will I offer burnt offerings unto the LORD my God of that which doth cost me nothing. So David bought the threshing floor and the oxen for fifty shekels of silver.

Therefore, the church leaders and the congregants must be willing and be prepared to pay for professional services. The design of the sanctuary can be printed and positioned where persons can easily see it and understand what the new church will look like. Also, with the use of multimedia and advanced technology, these artistic drawings can be displayed during church services, probably during the announcements.

Designing the floor plan and the layout of the building is very important. If the church leaders need to expand the building a few years later, then that information must be provided to the architect so that the floor plan's foundation will be designed and developed to allow future extension. The inner space must be properly utilized, making sure that there is adequate seating space for the congregants. If there is a need for children's church and training areas, all of that must be included in the design of the building. Some church leaders may request an area where the choir will be able to stand and sing on a regular basis.

Once the architectural design is completed and approved by the leadership in the church, then that will be the final building to be constructed. There are times when leaders may want to make changes, but major external changes at this point will compromise the integrity of the structure. For example, if the sanctuary was only designed as a one-flat building, then adding another flat will put more weight on the foundation beyond its capacity, which may cause the foundation to sink, shift, or crack.

9.3 Engineer's estimates

After the architectural design is completed, then the engineering estimate must be produced. There are several software programs that can assist with the design of buildings and produce the engineer's estimate. It is important that the data is entered into the software accurately so as to produce a reasonable estimate.

The engineer's estimate will guide the church leadership on the estimated amount of money needed to complete the sanctuary. Based upon the cost, if the church has enough funds, then they can start the construction at the earliest moment. If there are insufficient funds, then the leaders can organize fundraising or seek a mortgage from a financial institution.

With the engineer's estimate, a decision can be made to start the construction in phases, beginning with the foundation, if all the money is not yet available.

9.4 Major initial costs associated with the establishment of a sanctuary

The approach taken to construct a house or office must also be given to the construction of a sanctuary for God's people. There are multiple significant costs involved in the construction of any major building, including that of a physical place for God's people to worship the Creator.

Figure 7. Major costs associated with establishing a church building

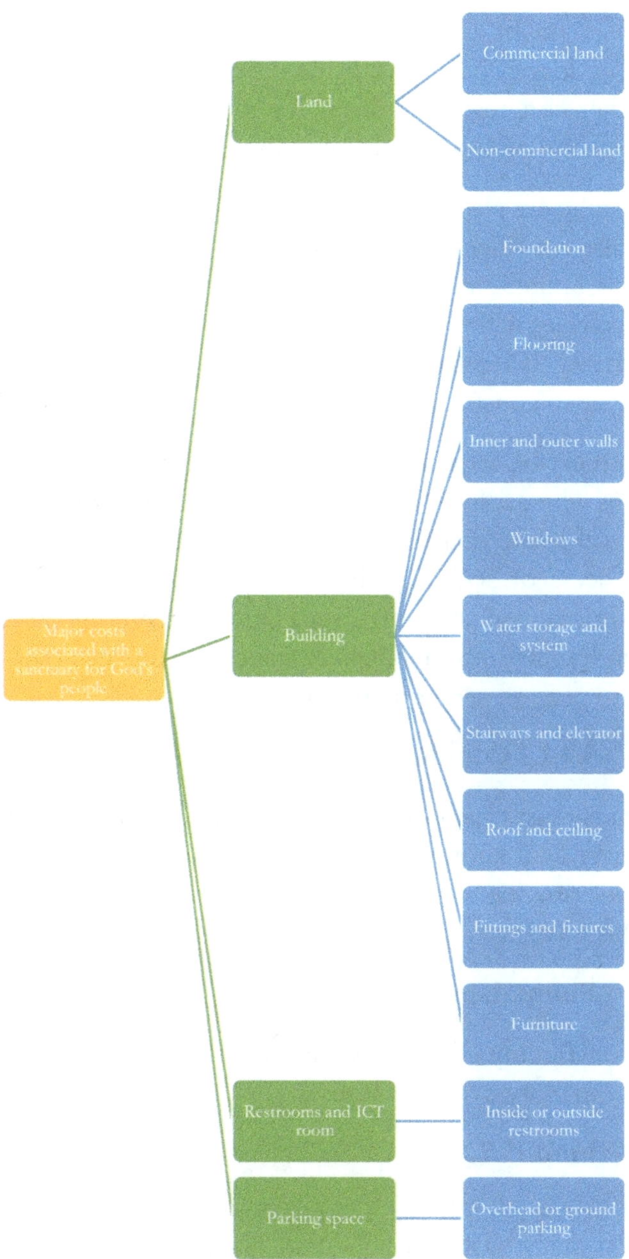

9.4.1 Land

If a new sanctuary will be established, then land will be needed. Some churches might already have started to construct at a particular location, so they have already identified and purchased the land. There are other congregations that have to acquire new lands to start the construction of God's place of worship.

Those who are responsible for acquiring lands to construct the church must also consider providing enough space for parking. When parking space is limited, many persons will not be able to comfortably park their vehicles within the church's space, so they may not want to join that church. Therefore, adequate parking space must be an important factor when considering acquiring land to erect a church building.

Lands must be acquired from legitimate landowners. There are some persons who are involved in the illegal sale of lands, so church leaders must make sure that they conduct due diligence before commencing the process of acquiring the land. It would be incorrect to misuse God's money on acquiring illegal land. When there are land disputes, church leaders must avoid such transactions, since they may lose the money spent on acquiring the land.

9.4.1.1 Commercial land

Believers must trust God for the best land to own and construct God's sanctuary. It is known that commercial lands are often expensive, but God will provide the money for his children if they trust him and work with his guidance.

Philippians 4:19

[19] But my God shall supply all your need according to his riches in glory by Christ Jesus.

John 15:7

[7] If ye abide in me, and my words abide in you, ye shall ask what ye will, and it shall be done unto you.

When commercial lands are acquired, the value of the land will appreciate over the years. With the acquisition of commercial lands, church leaders also have the opportunity to be in prominent locations to attract intelligent and financially stable persons. People must not see the church only as a place where the poor and illiterate persons will attend, but also where some of the most wealthy and intelligent persons will attend to hear from God and be touched by his presence.

9.4.1.2 Non-commercial land

If leaders are unable to acquire commercial lands, then they can acquire non-commercial lands, which will be available for lower costs. Oftentimes, non-commercial lands are in rural areas.

If the strategy of the church leaders is to build churches in different areas, especially rural areas, then they will have to acquire non-commercial lands. Many times, non-commercial lands will be larger and cost less money. This may allow the leaders to construct a larger sanctuary because they have more space, and the cost to construct the building will also be less.

9.4.2 Building

Once the leader has identified and possessed the lands, then it is time to start the construction of the building, as long as they have enough money. Most times, the construction of the building will be greater than the cost to acquire the land.

Children of God, go ahead and erect a sanctuary for the people of God to have a comfortable and stable place to meet and serve the Lord. Some church leaders are renting places for their weekly church services. However, it may be time for them to move on and own the building that they will now call their church, where they will meet and have regular fellowship with other believers and with the Lord.

9.4.2.1 Foundation

People oftentimes do not see the foundation, but even the most beautiful building needs a foundation to rest upon. Jesus, in his teaching, clearly mentions the foundation of the building in Luke

14:29. He knows that persons who need to erect a building must start from the foundation and then advance to the other parts of the building.

These are some important things that must be considered for the foundation of any building: for example, the soil type, the water table fluctuation, the number of flats that the building will have, the maximum amount of persons to be in the building at any given time, erosion, etc. These important things will guide the engineers to identify the costs to erect the church. If leaders want the church building to have several stories, then the foundation must be designed and prepared to accommodate that weight. If vehicles are to be parked on top of the building, then that will also affect the cost of the foundation.

If there is a need for elevators, then the cost for the foundation must reflect that. If the soil is very loose and will possibly shift, then driving piles in the earth as part of the foundation work will be necessary.

Leaders must remember that if they do not invest sufficient money for the foundation, then it may shift or crack, meaning that they will have to construct another building later. The work to be done on the foundation cannot be hurried. Sometimes, the soil must be compacted or given some time to settle and to bear the weight of the building.

If all the money is not immediately available but the leaders are confident that they will have the remaining funds soon, then they can proceed with the foundation. In a mountainous area or sandy soil, the cost of the foundation will be different from a building of the same dimension constructed in a clay area. With a good design and laid-out foundation, the building will remain intact for many decades. Persons must remember that the foundation cannot be adjusted after the building is erect, so give much time and money to a good foundation.

9.4.2.2 Flooring

The floor of the building will facilitate persons walking into and out of the church, and it allows persons to rest their feet while they are seated. Also, the furniture will rest on the church floor.

If the church floor is tiled, then the contractor must use nonskid tiles in order to allow persons to walk without sustaining injuries. In cases where nonskid tiles are not used, persons may trip and fall, which may cause severe injuries.

In countries and communities where flooding and earthquakes occur frequently, the design of the floor must factor in those natural environmental conditions.

9.4.2.3 Inner and outer walls

After the foundation is laid, then the outer and inner walls will be erected. The main material that people use for walls are wood, cement, and steel. These materials provide the strength needed for strong external walls. The internal walls can be erected with other building materials.

Strong external walls prevent vandals from defacing the building, sounds from entering the building, external hot or cold air from affecting persons inside the building, etc. Oftentimes, the external walls are more costly than the internal walls, based upon the design that is selected.

The external walls, columns, or steel structure must be strong enough to maintain the weight of the roof and ceiling. There may not be any beauty in the external walls, but those walls are very important to the building.

Many leaders would like to a fashionable or modern design for the internal walls. Some internal walls may be easy to adjust if leaders want to make any changes to the inner part of the building.

9.4.2.4 Painting

Painting the walls is another cost that must be considered in the estimate. Oil-based paints are more expensive than water-based paints. The color of paint for the inner and outer walls must be carefully considered, as leaders may want to use colors that support and highlight certain parts of the building. The lighting and color of a building often have a great impact on the eyes and minds of people.

9.4.2.5 Windows

The color, design, and material of the windows will impact the overall costs of the building. If leaders want sunlight to enter the building during certain times of the day, then the choice of windows will be important. Some special windows will enhance the look of the building. In countries where there are hurricanes, storms, and winter weather, then the choice of windows will be important.

9.4.2.6 Water storage and system

Any church building, whether small or large, needs running water. It is not guaranteed that running water will also flow through the main facilities established by the government. Therefore, storage of water will be important in the event of a water shortage from the government service. In times of earthquakes and hurricanes, the government water system may be disrupted for a few hours or days.

The design of the water storage can allow water vessels to be stored on the ground floor, trestles, or roof of the building. Any of these options will affect the final cost of the church building.

9.4.2.7 Stairways and elevator

The design of the stairways is very important. The building must have at least two doors. If one door is used as the entrance, then it must be clearly marked and identified for the congregants. If another door in a different location is used for the exit, then there must be a clear sign marked in the appropriate color to guide persons.

The stairways must be constructed to allow persons to easily move from one part of the building to another. If two persons have to use a stairway at the same time, then they must have easy access to move along the stairway together.

The design of the doors and stairways must have enough space to allow for furniture and other items to easily enter and be removed from the building. For example, the doors and stairways must be wide enough to allow chairs and tables to go in and out of the church. If musical instruments have to be placed in the church, then there must be enough space for them to get inside.

The stairway must be strong enough that in the event of an emergency, many persons will be able to use the same stairway at the same time. Many persons will use the stairways all at once when services are over as well.

Elevators will be necessary if the building has more than one flat. In the design of the building, it is important to know if elevators will be needed.

The new church must allow for disabled persons to independently enter and exit the building. Some disabled persons have not attended certain churches because the entrance and exit of the building were not designed for them to use wheelchairs or walkers.

If the building is tall, then it will be important to have rails along the stairway. These rails will allow persons to hold on to them as they walk up and down the stairway.

9.4.2.8 Roof and ceiling

The construction and design of the roof and ceiling must prevent too much heat from getting inside the building. In tropical countries, the roof will have to be designed differently than in countries with winter weather.

Flat or high roofs give different looks to the building. In cases where vehicles will have to park on the rooftop of the building, then the roof must be strong and designed to accommodate the weight of those vehicles. Most roofing materials are concrete, steel, zinc, shingle, etc.

Most modern churches have established ceilings in the church to add value to the building, but also, importantly, to prevent the noise within the church from affecting persons who are not in the building. Some churches have been charged under noise nuisance laws for excessive noise.

The lighting in the building is also important, so the roof must facilitate the type of lighting that the leaders need. If the leaders want to install air conditioner units in the building, then the ceiling and the roof will be important. It is good to have air conditioner units to regulate the temperature inside the building. During winter, the heat of the church will need to be on. In the summer, the inside of the church will need to be cool to make persons comfortable while attending the service.

A well-designed roof will add value to the building. When persons look at the building and even the ceiling, they must love the work done by the leaders and members of the church.

Guttering will be important for buildings that are not designed for vehicles to park on the rooftop. For example, buildings that have zinc and shingle roofs will often have gutters to trap and redirect the rainwater. Some churches may have a water storage facility to collect rainwater.

9.4.2.9 Fittings and fixtures

The fittings for some church buildings may be very costly, depending upon what the leaders and members want the finished church to look like. The layout of the electrical wires is important for the safety of all persons. Water will be needed in the building, so the layout of the pipes is also important.

If the church does not possess air conditioner units at the initial stage, then it may be important to install wall and ceiling fans. For large church buildings, there may be the need to have more than one at different places in the building.

9.4.2.10 Furniture

Acquiring furniture for the church must not be left to one person to do. The color and size of the furniture are important considerations for those who are responsible for acquiring them. Because persons will spend at least one hour sitting during the service time, the furniture must be comfortable for them. The furniture must be durable enough, since leaders are not expecting to replace it every year.

The furniture acquired must cater to the weight of different persons, since persons will take whatever seat is available to them if they are to choose their own seats. No leader will want to know that someone fell through the seat because it could not contain the weight of an average-size person.

The layout of the furniture is very important to allow persons to have easy access into and out of their seats. If the space is too narrow, then some persons will not be comfortable sitting in their seats.

If tables are needed for the fellowship hall and cafeteria areas of the church, then suitable tables must be purchased. Once again, if the leaders and members are working with a color scheme, then the color of the table must be carefully considered. The heights of tables for children will be different from those for toddlers.

9.4.3 Restrooms and ICT room

Most modern churches have to involve Information Communication and Technology (ICT) in their services. Because many church services are live streamed or recorded, then there is a need to have a media room to facilitate this essential service. Many persons may not be able to attend all of the church services, but if the services are recorded, then they can watch and listen to them at a later time. If leaders want to make the words of the worship songs visible to the congregants, then the facility must provide for that service. There are some leaders who will also make their sermons visible to the congregants while they are preaching. Some large churches have multimedia teams that will be responsible for ICT-related matters.

9.4.3.1 Inside or outside restrooms

Restrooms are essential for everyone and must be part of the construction of the building. There must be enough restrooms for the persons attending church services. When designing the church building, leaders must decide if they want the restrooms to be inside or outside of the building. At some churches, the restrooms will be in an adjacent building but within short walking distance from the main sanctuary.

When designing restrooms, persons must cater for children to use those facilities. If it is possible, separate restrooms can be construction for children, since their height will be different from that of most adults.

9.4.4 Parking space

It is almost impossible these days to build a church without space for parking. The size of the parking space will be different for each church, since it depends upon the size of the land they own.

In some places, if the soil is very solid, then leaders may not have much work to do to make parking space available. In other places, leaders will have to construct the parking space by making the foundation out of concrete.

The parking space must be properly laid out. Adequate space must be allocated for the ingress and egress of persons using it.

9.4.4.1 Overhead or ground parking

When the architect is designing the building and the parking, they must know if parking will be done on the ground around the church building or on the roof of the building. This information is critical for the design of the building and the associated costs. Once the space is designed for parking, then guidance must be provided about whether parallel, double parking, etc., will be most appropriate for the parking space.

10. Operational and maintenance costs for the new building

After the building is completed, there will be some operational or running costs. These are recurring costs that are directly associated with the building. Some persons are fascinated with the elegant look of a building but do not give much attention to the fact that there are other costs involved in maintaining it.

10.1 Janitors

Leaders must consider janitorial services for the church. The larger the building, the more cost and time will be taken to keep it clean. Sometimes, volunteer service can be offered to keep the church clean. Leaders must ensure that they have a permanent and reliable system of ensuring that the church is cleaned properly and on time.

When persons volunteer their service, it is not always certain that they will give their best service at all times. At some large churches, the janitorial service is outsourced to companies. Some church leaders will agree to pay certain members for cleaning the church, as they see this as an opportunity to provide employment to their members and to keep the money within the church.

10.2 Insurance

It will be risky to have an expensive church building and no insurance. Fire, floods, and hurricanes do not provide advance notice when they occur. Therefore, leaders must ensure that the church buildings are properly insured. The insurance policy must cover the true cost of the building and its contents. It may be important to evaluate the building every five or ten years and adjust the insurance coverage so as to ensure that if they have to recover any money from the insurance company, they will receive close to the market value for the buildings and its contents.

10.3 Utility services

Once a building is erected and operationalized, then there will be utility costs. If the church does not possess its own generator or solar electricity system, then it will have to depend on electricity from the national grid. Therefore, regular payments will have to be made for the consumption of electricity. Many churches also depend upon external water supplies, which will result in having to pay for water services.

The telephone is another utility service that cannot be ignored. Many churches will have an administrative office that will be staffed by church members or other professional persons. These individuals will have to make telephone calls on behalf of the church, and as such, telephone costs will be incurred.

To physically secure the assets in the church, there will be the need for a security officer or firm. Security costs will be paid weekly, fortnightly, or monthly. While some church members can provide security services, it is important that the church have reliable and capable persons to secure the church's assets.

10.4 Parking lot officer

If the church has designated parking spaces, then someone or several persons may be required to direct drivers in and out of the parking areas. Those who provide this service are expected to be paid on a consistent basis.

The work of the Lord will always cost someone. Therefore, those who are committed to doing the work of the Lord must be willing to make sacrifices and manage the financial resources that God has placed into their care.

11. Project financing

The costs to construct new churches may be large for some congregations. Therefore, once they agree to proceed with this project, then they need to secure enough funds. The leaders and members can consider internal financing or borrowing.

Many leaders would like to generate funds internally to construct the church. This is possible, but it can take a long time for some churches.

Figure 8. Generating funds internally to build a new church

Many leaders can be more comfortable seeking financing from members of their congregation to generate funds to erect a new church building. This can be a good idea, since they do not have to repay any person or institution.

With the strategic plan to establish churches, leaders will work within their budget to generate the funds needed. Concerts and takeaway lunches on a regular basis, for example, can generate needed funds for the church. Members are sometimes willing to make pledges that they will contribute specific amounts to the church. There are some organizations that will engage in corporate sponsorship of churches that participate in community development.

Most of the internal sources of financing have one common disadvantage, which is the length of time it may take to garner the funds. Nevertheless, members must be encouraged to give to the work of the Lord.

11.1 The people's contribution

When the tabernacle of the Lord had to be built, God gave Moses specific guidance on what had to be done. Moses was now tasked with building and furnishing the tabernacle, and he needed resources to get the work done. He then turned to the people of God for them to give. He did not force them to give, since they were expected to give from a willing heart.

Exodus 35:4-29

4 And Moses spake unto all the congregation of the children of Israel, saying, This is the thing which the LORD commanded, saying, 5 Take ye from among you an offering unto the LORD: whosoever is of a willing heart, let him bring it, an offering of the LORD; gold, and silver, and brass, 6 And blue, and purple, and scarlet, and fine linen, and goats' hair, 7 And rams' skins dyed red, and badgers' skins, and shittim wood, 8 And oil for the light, and spices for anointing oil, and for the sweet incense, 9 And onyx stones, and stones to be set for the ephod, and for the breastplate.

10 And every wise hearted among you shall come, and make all that the LORD hath commanded; 11 The tabernacle, his tent, and his covering, his taches, and his boards, his bars, his pillars, and his sockets, 12 The ark, and the staves thereof, with the mercy seat, and the vail of the covering, 13 The table, and his staves, and all his vessels, and the shewbread, 14 The candlestick

also for the light, and his furniture, and his lamps, with the oil for the light, 15 And the incense altar, and his staves, and the anointing oil, and the sweet incense, and the hanging for the door at the entering in of the tabernacle, 16 The altar of burnt offering, with his brasen grate, his staves, and all his vessels, the laver and his foot, 17 The hangings of the court, his pillars, and their sockets, and the hanging for the door of the court, 18 The pins of the tabernacle, and the pins of the court, and their cords, 19 The cloths of service, to do service in the holy place, the holy garments for Aaron the priest, and the garments of his sons, to minister in the priest's office.

20 And all the congregation of the children of Israel departed from the presence of Moses. 21 And they came, every one whose heart stirred him up, and every one whom his spirit made willing, and they brought the LORD's offering to the work of the tabernacle of the congregation, and for all his service, and for the holy garments. 22 And they came, both men and women, as many as were willing hearted, and brought bracelets, and earrings, and rings, and tablets, all jewels of gold: and every man that offered offered an offering of gold unto the LORD. 23 And every man, with whom was found blue, and purple, and scarlet, and fine linen, and goats' hair, and red skins of rams, and badgers' skins, brought them. 24 Every one that did offer an offering of silver and brass brought the LORD's offering: and every man, with whom was found shittim wood for any work of the service, brought it. 25 And all the women that were wise hearted did spin with their hands, and brought that which they had spun, both of blue, and of purple, and of scarlet, and of fine linen. 26 And all the women whose heart stirred them up in wisdom spun goats' hair. 27 And the rulers brought onyx stones, and stones to be set, for the ephod, and for the breastplate; 28 And spice, and oil for the light, and for the anointing oil, and for the sweet incense. 29 The children of Israel brought a willing offering unto the LORD, every man and woman, whose heart made them willing to bring for all manner

> of work, which the LORD had commanded to be made by the hand of Moses.

It is so encouraging to see that the congregation heeded Moses's request to make contributions to the work of the Lord. Many leaders would like to have members like those Israelites that Moses had in Exodus 35:4-29. In many congregations, there are faithful members and visitors who will give generously to the works of the Lord.

11.2 The congregants gave more than was needed

After Moses asked the people of God to give, they were happy and continuously brought resources to start and complete the construction of the tabernacle. When Moses heard from Bezaleel and Aholiab about how much the people had given and that their giving exceeded what was needed, Moses commanded the people to cease giving. Thanks be to God that the people of God were able to self-finance the tabernacle of God.

> **Exodus 36:1-7**
>
> [1]Then wrought Bezaleel and Aholiab, and every wise hearted
> man, in whom the LORD put wisdom and understanding to
> know how to work all manner of work for the service of the
> sanctuary, according to all that the LORD had commanded.
> [2]And Moses called Bezaleel and Aholiab, and every wise
> hearted man, in whose heart the LORD had put wisdom, even
> every one whose heart stirred him up to come unto the work
> to do it: [3]And they received of Moses all the offering, which
> the children of Israel had brought for the work of the service
> of the sanctuary, to make it withal. And they brought yet unto
> him free offerings every morning. [4]And all the wise men, that
> wrought all the work of the sanctuary, came every man from
> his work which they made; [5]And they spake unto Moses,
> saying, The people bring much more than enough for the
> service of the work, which the LORD commanded to make.
> [6]And Moses gave commandment, and they caused it to be
> proclaimed throughout the camp, saying, Let neither man nor
> woman make any more work for the offering of the sanctuary.

> So the people were restrained from bringing. [7] For the stuff they had was sufficient for all the work to make it, and too much.

11.3 Borrowing

A leader can arrange to borrow money for the work of the Lord. The work they want to do for God may be urgent, and they may already perceive that the congregants will not be able to make substantial financial contributions in a timely manner. God does not hate people when they borrow, but he hates when people choose not to repay what they have borrowed.

> Borrowers . . . need money to finance their purchases. This includes businesses that need money to finance their investments or to expand their inventories as well as individuals who borrow money to purchase a new car or a new home. (Titman et al., 2016)

There are many financial institutions that are constantly offering loans and mortgages to persons, some of whom will gladly take up those offers. However, when they approach those financial institutions, they will have to provide many documents. Before seeking financing, persons must consider the following factors.

Figure 9. Factors to consider when borrowing

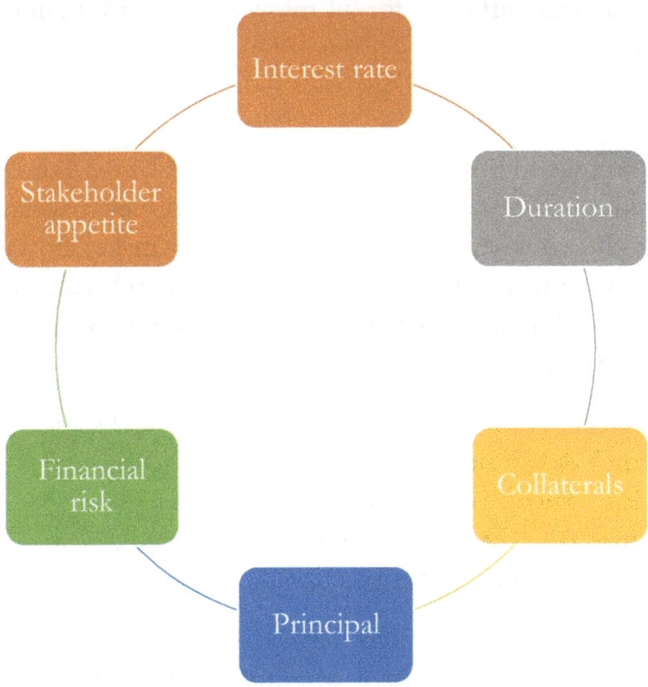

Funding the initial down payment may be a problem for some persons and churches. Once funds are borrowed, then regular installments will have to be made until the financing period has ended.

Before signing the financing agreement, the prospective borrower must assess the interest rate. While the funds can be easily available to persons, the interest rate may be significant, and the borrower may be repaying large installments until the loan is fully repaid.

> [The interest] rate is the price paid (by the borrower) for the loan of money (made by the lender). (Lane, 1966)

For a short duration, such as a period of one year or less, the financial institution may offer simple interest. However, if the duration is longer, then compound interest may be applied, which means that the borrower has to repay more funds to the financial institution.

Before loans or mortgages are approved, the client will have to provide something as collateral. If they do not have collateral, then their loan application will not be processed.

Figure 10. Collateral required by lending institutions

If the church leaders have land transport, then they have one important legal document that many financial institutions often require. The transport or lease will have to be lodged with the financial institution until the full amount is repaid.

Persons and organizations who are seeking financing will often have to disclose much of their personal financial information, such as their source of income, frequency of income, savings accounts, etc. Borrowing allows for people to have the money they need, but they must be disciplined enough to spend it on the things that they planned for, and to repay the principal and interest on time.

12. Supporting new churches financially

The parent church or sending church must allocate funds to assist the new church leaders and the work of the Lord at the new church. When a new church is established, it may be challenging for the new leaders to find sufficient money to manage the expenses involved. These new leaders will need every possible source of financial help that they can get.

Sometimes, an entire family may be appointed to the new church, and their source of income may not be sufficient to provide for themselves and the work of the Lord. New churches may take some time to attract and then retain new members.

If, at the beginning, a specific allowance is offered to the new church leaders, it may be a good start. Probably within the year, the amount of the allowance can be reduced and eventually cease once the leaders are generating enough funds from the new church.

The work of the Lord requires money, and God expects those who are able to give to those who have a need. Even small contributions from several persons will make a great impact on those who need such support.

Acts 4:34-35

> 34 Neither was there any among them that lacked: for as many as were possessors of lands or houses sold them, and brought the prices of the things that were sold, 35 And laid them down at the apostles' feet: and distribution was made unto every man according as he had need.

After Jesus was ascended, the apostles continued to share God's word with others. There were needs among them, and those who had possessions were willing to provide for the needs of fellow believers. God was among them and kept adding to the church. God is always willing to add souls to the church when believers walk in love.

Acts 2:44-47

> 44 And all that believed were together, and had all things common; 45 And sold their possessions and goods, and parted them to all men, as every man had need. 46 And they, continuing daily with one accord in the temple, and breaking bread from house to house, did eat their meat with gladness and singleness of heart, 47 Praising God, and having favour with all the people. And the Lord added to the church daily such as should be saved.

There are some believers who need to practice giving to the work of the Lord and toward new churches that they are associated with. When everyone gives, it helps the work of the Lord to continue to reach the lives of many persons.

2 Corinthians 9:10-15

> 10 Now he that ministereth seed to the sower both minister bread for your food, and multiply your seed sown, and increase the fruits of your righteousness; 11 Being enriched in everything to all bountifulness, which causeth through us thanksgiving to God. 12 For the administration of this service not only supplieth the want of the saints, but is abundant also by many thanksgivings unto God; 13 Whiles by the experiment of this ministration they glorify God for your professed subjection unto the gospel of Christ, and for your liberal distribution unto them, and unto all men; 14 And by their prayer for you, which long after you for the exceeding grace of God in you. 15 Thanks be unto God for his unspeakable gift.

God often blesses those who give. Those who do not like to give will only affect their own blessings.

Proverbs 11:24-25

> [24] There is that scattereth, and yet increaseth; and there is that withholdeth more than is meet, but it tendeth to poverty. [25] The liberal soul shall be made fat: and he that watereth shall be watered also himself.

The Apostle Paul also sees the need for the rich people of this world to contribute financially to the things of God. Believers must let the rich know that when they give toward the Lord's work, they are doing something good for themselves.

1 Timothy 6:17-19

> [17] Charge them that are rich in this world, that they be not high minded, nor trust in uncertain riches, but in the living God, who giveth us richly all things to enjoy; [18] That they do good, that they be rich in good works, ready to distribute, willing to communicate; [19] Laying up in store for themselves a good foundation against the time to come, that they may lay hold on eternal life.

13. Utilizing skilled workers and quality materials

When a church building has to be erected, skilled workers must be sought for this important project. If part of the labor force is unskilled, at least those who are involved in the major tasks must be technical enough to start and finish the work.

In trying to keep costs minimal, leaders must avoid compromising the quality of the work. If the leaders award the contract to a professional firm, then they can ask for the qualifications and background of all persons who will be involved in the construction of the building. Leaders have the right to ask for such information because they are spending God's money to complete an important building.

13.1 Moses utilized skilled workers

Some church leaders will utilize members of the congregation to construct the new building. However, those members must possess the necessary skills to build the house of God. When Moses had to build the tabernacle, he used technical and skilled workers.

> **Exodus 35:30-35**
>
> 30 And Moses said unto the children of Israel, See,
> the LORD hath called by name Bezaleel, the son of Uri, the son
> of Hur, of the tribe of Judah; 31 And he hath filled him with the
> spirit of God, in wisdom, in understanding, and in knowledge,
> and in all manner of workmanship; 32 And to devise curious
> works, to work in gold, and in silver, and in brass, 33 And in the
> cutting of stones, to set them, and in carving of wood, to make
> any manner of cunning work. 34 And he hath put in his heart
> that he may teach, both he, and Aholiab, the son of Ahisamach,
> of the tribe of Dan. 35 Them hath he filled with wisdom of

> heart, to work all manner of work, of the engraver, and of the cunning workman, and of the embroiderer, in blue, and in purple, in scarlet, and in fine linen, and of the weaver, even of them that do any work, and of those that devise cunning work.

Those who were in charge of the project came and provided Moses with a report of the work that was done. Moses relied on them because they were technical persons. When church leaders find technical persons, they must allow them to perform their professional work.

13.2 King Solomon utilized skilled workers and quality building materials

King David wanted to build the temple of God, but God rejected his offer (1 Chronicles 28:3). However, God decided to make the name of King David great. Even today, many persons remember King David. Oftentimes, when Jesus is mentioned, persons will refer to him as "Son of David," because Jesus came through the lineage of King David.

King Solomon, a son of David, was given the opportunity to build the first temple of God. He was very selective in building the house of God, as he chose quality materials and skilled workers.

> **2 Chronicles 2:1-18**
>
> [1] And Solomon determined to build an house for the name of the LORD, and an house for his kingdom. [2] And Solomon told out threescore and ten thousand men to bear burdens, and fourscore thousand to hew in the mountain, and three thousand and six hundred to oversee them. [3] And Solomon sent to Huram the king of Tyre, saying, As thou didst deal with David my father, and didst send him cedars to build him an house to dwell therein, even so deal with me. [4] Behold, I build an house to the name of the LORD my God, to dedicate it to him, and to burn before him sweet incense, and for the continual shewbread, and for the burnt offerings morning and evening, on the sabbaths, and on the new moons, and on the solemn feasts of the LORD our God. This is an ordinance for ever to Israel. [5] And the house which I build is great: for great

is our God above all gods. 6 But who is able to build him an house, seeing the heaven and heaven of heavens cannot contain him? who am I then, that I should build him an house, save only to burn sacrifice before him?

7 Send me now therefore a man cunning to work in gold, and in silver, and in brass, and in iron, and in purple, and crimson, and blue, and that can skill to grave with the cunning men that are with me in Judah and in Jerusalem, whom David my father did provide. 8 Send me also cedar trees, fir trees, and algum trees, out of Lebanon: for I know that thy servants can skill to cut timber in Lebanon; and, behold, my servants shall be with thy servants, 9 Even to prepare me timber in abundance: for the house which I am about to build shall be wonderful great. 10 And, behold, I will give to thy servants, the hewers that cut timber, twenty thousand measures of beaten wheat, and twenty thousand measures of barley, and twenty thousand baths of wine, and twenty thousand baths of oil.

11 Then Huram the king of Tyre answered in writing, which he sent to Solomon, Because the LORD hath loved his people, he hath made thee king over them. 12 Huram said moreover, Blessed be the LORD God of Israel, that made heaven and earth, who hath given to David the king a wise son, endued with prudence and understanding, that might build an house for the LORD, and an house for his kingdom. 13 And now I have sent a cunning man, endued with understanding, of Huram my father's, 14 The son of a woman of the daughters of Dan, and his father was a man of Tyre, skilful to work in gold, and in silver, in brass, in iron, in stone, and in timber, in purple, in blue, and in fine linen, and in crimson; also to grave any manner of graving, and to find out every device which shall be put to him, with thy cunning men, and with the cunning men of my lord David thy father.

15 Now therefore the wheat, and the barley, the oil, and the wine, which my lord hath spoken of, let him send unto his servants: 16 And we will cut wood out of Lebanon, as much as

> thou shalt need: and we will bring it to thee in floats by sea to Joppa; and thou shalt carry it up to Jerusalem. [17] And Solomon numbered all the strangers that were in the land of Israel, after the numbering wherewith David his father had numbered them; and they were found an hundred and fifty thousand and three thousand and six hundred. [18] And he set threescore and ten thousand of them to be bearers of burdens, and fourscore thousand to be hewers in the mountain, and three thousand and six hundred overseers to set the people a work.

This shows that King Solomon was prepared to give the best to God. It took King Solomon seven years to complete the temple, but he was satisfied with the quality of work that he received (1 Kings 6:38). The people who were involved in the construction of the building did not work full time on it, because they had other duties to perform; otherwise, the work would have been completed in a shorter duration.

Modern-day church leaders must follow the examples of Moses and King Solomon to make sure that they utilize quality building materials to build God's house. The workers must have the skills and technical capability to start and complete the work of the Lord.

14. Members working together as one

The work of the Lord cannot be done by one individual. One of the reasons some new church leaders have failed after being assigned to new churches is that they had to perform almost every activity at the new churches. Whenever leaders are sent to new churches, they must have enough human support with them to execute God's work. God is a spirit, and he is able to do as much as he wants, but human beings need the support of each other.

14.1 Jethro taught Moses about delegation

God called Moses to lead his people. This was a new and exciting thing for Moses to do. Moses was happy with this calling, and he did what he knew best. However, his father-in-law saw that while Moses had the zeal of God, he needed wisdom in order to be effective in his execution of his assignment. His father-in-law had a discussion with him and shared with him the need to have more persons working along with him to execute the work of the Lord. Moses, being a wise son-in-law, took the advice of his father-in-law and appointed other persons to perform some of the tasks that he was toiling hard each day to get done.

An important lesson is learned here: team effort will produce greater results. Therefore, many senior church leaders need to allow more persons to work for the Lord, since God's works can be done through many persons who have his Spirit and depend upon him for guidance.

Exodus 18:17-27

17 And Moses' father in law said unto him, The thing that thou
doest is not good. 18 Thou wilt surely wear away, both thou, and
this people that is with thee: for this thing is too heavy for thee;

thou art not able to perform it thyself alone. [19] Hearken now
unto my voice, I will give thee counsel, and God shall be with
thee: Be thou for the people to God-ward, that thou mayest
bring the causes unto God: [20] And thou shalt teach them
ordinances and laws, and shalt shew them the way wherein they
must walk, and the work that they must do. [21] Moreover thou
shalt provide out of all the people able men, such as fear God,
men of truth, hating covetousness; and place such over them,
to be rulers of thousands, and rulers of hundreds, rulers of
fifties, and rulers of tens: [22] And let them judge the people at all
seasons: and it shall be, that every great matter they shall bring
unto thee, but every small matter they shall judge: so shall it be
easier for thyself, and they shall bear the burden with thee. [23] If
thou shalt do this thing, and God command thee so, then thou
shalt be able to endure, and all this people shall also go to their
place in peace.

[24] So Moses hearkened to the voice of his father in law, and did
all that he had said. [25] And Moses chose able men out of all
Israel, and made them heads over the people, rulers of
thousands, rulers of hundreds, rulers of fifties, and rulers of
tens. [26] And they judged the people at all seasons: the hard
causes they brought unto Moses, but every small matter they
judged themselves. [27] And Moses let his father in law depart;
and he went his way into his own land.

Figure 11. New hierarchy structure of Moses's leadership (Exodus 18:21)

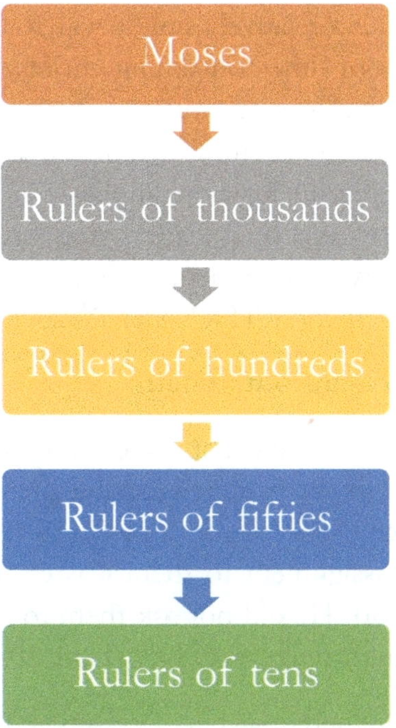

Jethro's advice brought great relief to Moses. Just imagine if Moses had to deal with thousands of people all by himself. He would become tired and die soon, and he would not be able to fulfill the plan of God for his life.

> Delegation is the process by which an individual manager or supervisor transfers part of his legitimate authority to a subordinate but without passing on the ultimate responsibility which has been entrusted to him by his own supervisor. (Cole, 1993)

Each senior church leader who is appointing leaders to pastor a new church must understand that support persons are needed for the new leaders. The new leaders must be taught delegation, just as Jethro taught Moses. Some believers think that delegation makes them less influential, but in the kingdom of God, there is no competition. God often likes his people to work in harmony as they fulfill his assignment for their lives.

> Delegation is a relatively simple way for leaders to free themselves of time-consuming chores, give followers developmental opportunities . . . and [increase] the number of tasks accomplished by the workgroup, team or committee. Delegation implies that someone has been empowered by a leader, boss or coach to take responsibility for completing certain tasks or engaging in certain activities. (Hughes et al., 2015)

14.2 Jesus sent persons out in pairs

Jesus, as a great leader, knew that he could not be at every place at the same time. Therefore, he gathered capable persons and sent them on a mission to preach, "The kingdom of God has come nigh unto you" (Luke 10:9). The assignment to them was clear, and they knew that they had his support. He did not ask them to be confrontational but to let peace prevail through their lives (Luke 10:5-8).

Take note, Jesus gathered seventy persons, but he sent them out in pairs (Luke 10:1). There was no restriction in terms of where they could go, since he sent them into every city and place (Luke 10:1). This therefore meant that Jesus had thirty-five pairs of persons (seventy divided by two), sent to different places to preach about the Kingdom of God.

> **Luke 10:1-23**
>
> 1 After these things the LORD appointed other seventy also,
> and sent them two and two before his face into every city and
> place, whither he himself would come. 2 Therefore said he unto
> them, The harvest truly is great, but the labourers are few: pray
> ye therefore the Lord of the harvest, that he would send forth
> labourers into his harvest. 3 Go your ways: behold, I send you
> forth as lambs among wolves. 4 Carry neither purse, nor scrip,
> nor shoes: and salute no man by the way. 5 And into
> whatsoever house ye enter, first say, Peace be to this house.

6 And if the son of peace be there, your peace shall rest upon it: if not, it shall turn to you again. 7 And in the same house remain, eating and drinking such things as they give: for the labourer is worthy of his hire. Go not from house to house. 8 And into whatsoever city ye enter, and they receive you, eat such things as are set before you: 9 And heal the sick that are therein, and say unto them, The kingdom of God is come nigh unto you.

10 But into whatsoever city ye enter, and they receive you not, go your ways out into the streets of the same, and say, 11 Even the very dust of your city, which cleaveth on us, we do wipe off against you: notwithstanding be ye sure of this, that the kingdom of God is come nigh unto you. 12 But I say unto you, that it shall be more tolerable in that day for Sodom, than for that city. 13 Woe unto thee, Chorazin! woe unto thee, Bethsaida! for if the mighty works had been done in Tyre and Sidon, which have been done in you, they had a great while ago repented, sitting in sackcloth and ashes. 14 But it shall be more tolerable for Tyre and Sidon at the judgment, than for you. 15 And thou, Capernaum, which art exalted to heaven, shalt be thrust down to hell. 16 He that heareth you heareth me; and he that despiseth you despiseth me; and he that despiseth me despiseth him that sent me.

17 And the seventy returned again with joy, saying, Lord, even the devils are subject unto us through thy name. 18 And he said unto them, I beheld Satan as lightning fall from heaven. 19 Behold, I give unto you power to tread on serpents and scorpions, and over all the power of the enemy: and nothing shall by any means hurt you. 20 Notwithstanding in this rejoice not, that the spirits are subject unto you; but rather rejoice, because your names are written in heaven.

21 In that hour Jesus rejoiced in spirit, and said, I thank thee, O Father, Lord of heaven and earth, that thou hast hid these things from the wise and prudent, and hast revealed them unto babes: even so, Father; for so it seemed good in thy sight. 22 All

things are delivered to me of my Father: and no man knoweth who the Son is, but the Father; and who the Father is, but the Son, and he to whom the Son will reveal him. [23] And he turned him unto his disciples, and said privately, Blessed are the eyes which see the things that ye see.

The seventy persons that Jesus sent out all returned to him and provided a progress report (Luke 10:17-19). One of the good practices that some new leaders do not always follow is providing feedback. They sometimes become so excited with what God is doing that they forget that they have reporting authority to follow.

Figure 12. Principles of effective delegation

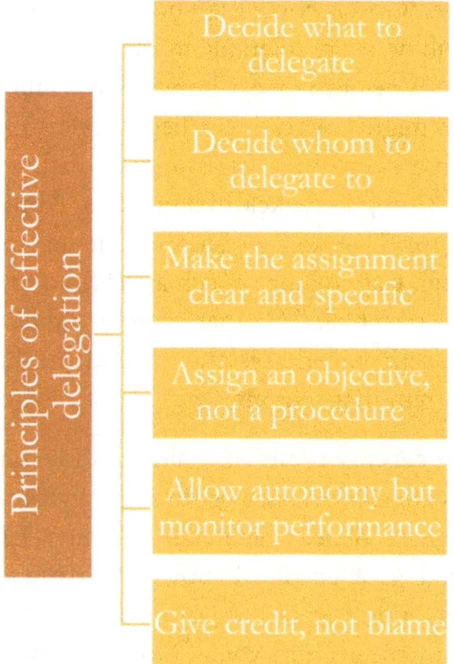

(Extracted from Hughes et al., 2015)

By sending them out in pairs, Jesus caused each person to be accountable to the other person in their group. This was very interesting, since it meant they were not all alone doing the work of the Lord.

The work of God needs the support of others, since each person has their own wisdom and abilities. When persons have the support of others, they can receive correction for the things they do wrong and praise for the good things they do.

New church leaders need support persons to work with. They must have enough persons to assist in different areas of ministry. When they have the support of others, the church can progress quickly and will continue to function effectively.

14.3 Agreement is important for success

Jesus taught an important lesson to his disciples about agreement. In his teaching, he let them know how impactful two persons can be. However, we must not limit this teaching of Jesus to mean that only two persons must be in agreement. Jesus wants the message to be clear to all that with two or more persons, great things can happen if they are in agreement. It will be better if even more persons agree to do the same thing.

> **Matthew 18:19**
>
> 19 Again I say unto you, That if two of you shall agree on earth as touching anything that they shall ask, it shall be done for them of my Father which is in heaven.

The apostles Paul and Silas were on a mission for God. After they cast out the evil spirit from the fortune teller, they were then accused by those who benefited from this lady's evil works. Eventually, the accuser of Paul and Silas took them to the magistrate, and they were put in prison.

As Paul and Silas agreed and spent time praying and singing, God heard them and was ready to deliver them. Their agreement, prayer, and singing caught the attention of a God who is always willing to defend his children.

> 25 And at midnight Paul and Silas prayed, and sang praises unto
> God: and the prisoners heard them. 26 And suddenly there was
> a great earthquake, so that the foundations of the prison were

shaken: and immediately all the doors were opened, and every one's bands were loosed.

Figure 13. God's impact when Paul and Silas agreed in prison

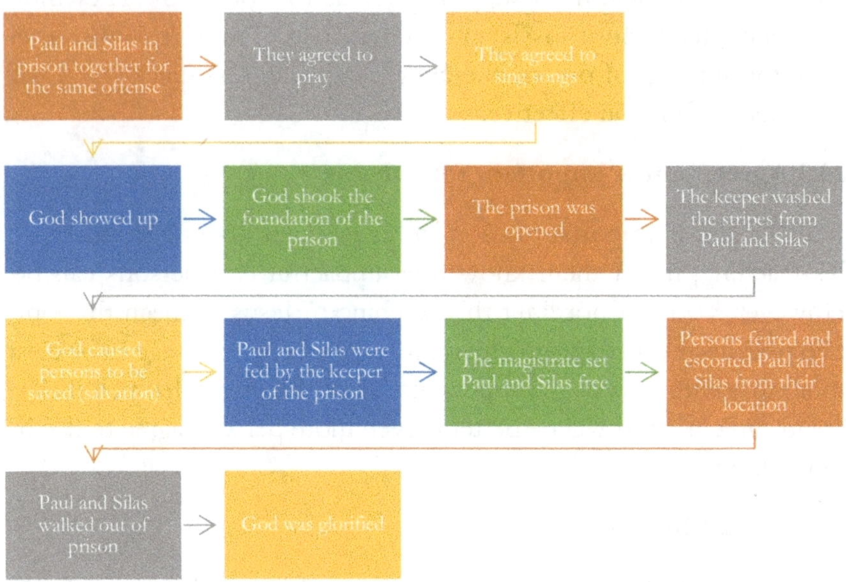

When senior leaders have allocated new leaders to take up appointments at new churches, they must send them with persons who will work as one. New leaders need less opposition from those who are supposed to be working with them. What they need is more team support.

Ecclesiastes 4:9-12

9 Two are better than one; because they have a good reward for their labour. 10 For if they fall, the one will lift up his fellow: but woe to him that is alone when he falleth; for he hath not another to help him up. 11 Again, if two lie together, then they have heat: but how can one be warm alone? 12 And if one prevail against him, two shall withstand him; and a threefold cord is not quickly broken.

Whenever one leader's spirits are down, they must find spiritual strength from their team member. Every leader will have challenges, but they are often strengthened when they have internal support.

15. Identifying potential church leaders

The establishment of a new church will demand that at least one leader be identified and appointed to start it. Some senior pastors would like to hold active positions at both the parent church and the new church. However, they will only burn themselves out, and they may not be effective in providing leadership to both congregations. Therefore, it is important to identify other persons who will carry out the plans of God at another location.

Every senior leader of God's work must remember that they do not own any church. They are only workers in God's vineyard.

15.1 Physical appearance and wealth are not a requirement for new leaders

When identifying potential new leaders, it is important to look for persons who have certain important qualities. These leaders must have a passion for the works of the Lord. However, other qualities should not be taken into account. For example, the height and size of the individuals must never be factors for consideration. A person's wealth also cannot be the determining factor for them to be given the opportunity to be identified and appointed as leaders in the new churches.

God wanted to anoint a king over Israel to replace King Saul, so he told the prophet Samuel to go to Jesse and anoint one of his sons (1 Samuel 16:1). When Samuel saw some of Jesse's eldest sons, he thought, based upon their appearance, that the older sons would be the prime candidates (1 Samuel 16:6-10). However, the Lord rejected those older sons of Jesse and instead agreed for David to be anointed and approved as the next king (1 Samuel 16:10-13). Many religious leaders must remember that God is looking at the heart and spirit of the new leader rather than their external appearance and wealth.

1 Samuel 16:1-13

1 And the LORD said unto Samuel, How long wilt thou mourn for Saul, seeing I have rejected him from reigning over Israel? fill thine horn with oil, and go, I will send thee to Jesse the Bethlehemite: for I have provided me a king among his sons. 2 And Samuel said, How can I go? if Saul hear it, he will kill me. And the LORD said, Take an heifer with thee, and say, I am come to sacrifice to the LORD. 3 And call Jesse to the sacrifice, and I will shew thee what thou shalt do: and thou shalt anoint unto me him whom I name unto thee. 4 And Samuel did that which the LORD spake, and came to Bethlehem. And the elders of the town trembled at his coming, and said, Comest thou peaceably? 5 And he said, Peaceably: I am come to sacrifice unto the LORD: sanctify yourselves, and come with me to the sacrifice. And he sanctified Jesse and his sons, and called them to the sacrifice. 6 And it came to pass, when they were come, that he looked on Eliab, and said, Surely the LORD's anointed is before him. 7 But the LORD said unto Samuel, Look not on his countenance, or on the height of his stature; because I have refused him: for the LORD seeth not as man seeth; for man looketh on the outward appearance, but the LORD looketh on the heart.

8 Then Jesse called Abinadab, and made him pass before Samuel. And he said, Neither hath the LORD chosen this. 9 Then Jesse made Shammah to pass by. And he said, Neither hath the LORD chosen this. 10 Again, Jesse made seven of his sons to pass before Samuel. And Samuel said unto Jesse, The LORD hath not chosen these. 11 And Samuel said unto Jesse, Are here all thy children? And he said, There remaineth yet the youngest, and, behold, he keepeth the sheep. And Samuel said unto Jesse, Send and fetch him: for we will not sit down till he come hither. 12 And he sent, and brought him in. Now he was ruddy, and withal of a beautiful countenance, and

> goodly to look to. And the LORD said, Arise, anoint him: for this is he. [13] Then Samuel took the horn of oil, and anointed him in the midst of his brethren: and the Spirit of the LORD came upon David from that day forward. So Samuel rose up, and went to Ramah.

It has become common practice in the church for leaders to select persons of wealth and position. Oftentimes, we have seen that those who have wealth and position in the secular world are biased and inexperienced when it comes to the things of God. Serving in the church shouldn't be for recognition. Those who truly have a heart for ministry will serve the people.

> **Matthew 20:25-26 (NKJV)**
>
> [25] But Jesus called them to Himself and said, "You know that the rulers of the Gentiles lord it over them, and those who are great exercise authority over them. [26] Yet it shall not be so among you; but whoever desires to become great among you, let him be your servant."

15.2 Potential leaders must have wisdom and God's Spirit

God wants to work through new leaders who have his Spirit and wisdom to lead his people. When new leaders do not have God's Spirit and wisdom, they often use force and threats to get people to work for the Lord.

In the early church, while the main leaders were occupied with the works of the Lord, there was a need for additional leaders to perform certain duties. The apostles agreed that more believers should be identified and appointed to perform those additional duties. However, those new leaders must have the Spirit of God in their lives.

Once quality leaders are appointed, then the senior leaders can be at ease, knowing that God will work through those new leaders to fulfill his will. Those new leaders will have to depend upon God for direction as they lead the new flock of God in a new location.

16. Special training for new church leaders

Believers who are identified and appointed as new leaders must receive training. Even if they have been members of a church for many years, they will need to receive specific training.

"Training is a planned effort to facilitate the learning of job-related knowledge, skills and behavior by employees" (Noe et al., 2015).

The duration of the training may vary from church to church, since some of these potential leaders might already have received some training from Bible College. However, they must be given hands-on training at their current church.

Figure 14. Areas of special training for new church leaders

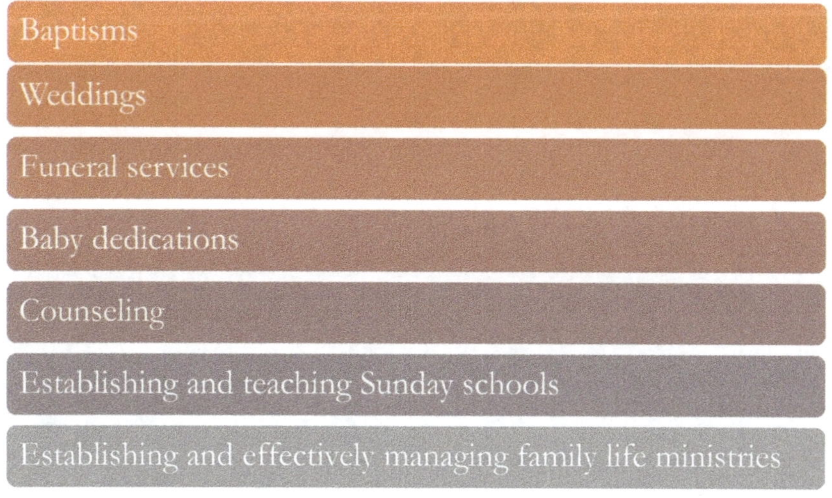

For different denominations, new leaders will have to receive different licenses to conduct some of these special services. For example, presiding over weddings may require special training, and the leader may have to complete special examinations.

Funeral services may also require new leaders to be provided with opportunities to practice. However, this area of special ministry may not require new leaders to write any examination.

Most upcoming leaders may already be involved in or have witnessed baby dedications and baptisms, so they may not need special training in these areas. Family life ministries will include men's and women's ministries, as well as youth ministry. New leaders may already be familiar with at least one of these family life ministries.

For counseling services, some churches will only use licensed counselors. This may be necessary, since counseling cannot be done by a novice. While a counselor may be good in one area of counseling, they may not be good in every area.

17. Appoint quality leaders

Those who are appointed as church leaders must have good qualities. Their lifestyles must set good examples for others. It is important that people follow Christian leaders not only because they are followers of Christ, but also because their lifestyles are good to follow. Their reputation must be a good testimony of them.

Titus 1:5-16

5 For this cause left I thee in Crete, that thou shouldest set in order the things that are wanting, and ordain elders in every city, as I had appointed thee: 6 If any be blameless, the husband of one wife, having faithful children not accused of riot or unruly. 7 For a bishop must be blameless, as the steward of God; not self-willed, not soon angry, not given to wine, no striker, not given to filthy lucre; 8 But a lover of hospitality, a lover of good men, sober, just, holy, temperate; 9 Holding fast the faithful word as he hath been taught, that he may be able by sound doctrine both to exhort and to convince the gainsayers.

10 For there are many unruly and vain talkers and deceivers, especially they of the circumcision: 11 Whose mouths must be stopped, who subvert whole houses, teaching things which they ought not, for filthy lucre's sake. 12 One of themselves, even a prophet of their own, said, the Cretians are alway liars, evil beasts, slow bellies. 13 This witness is true. Wherefore rebuke them sharply, that they may be sound in the faith; 14 Not giving heed to Jewish fables, and commandments of men, that turn from the truth.

15 Unto the pure all things are pure: but unto them that are defiled and unbelieving is nothing pure; but even their mind

> and conscience is defiled. [16] They profess that they know God; but in works they deny him, being abominable, and disobedient, and unto every good work reprobate.

Titus 1:5 tells us that leaders must be appointed to perform the duties of God. It is clear that these leaders must be ordained and appointed to these positions. Therefore, when new churches are established, persons must be appointed to lead those churches and not just sent as ordinary members. When leaders recognize that they are valued, they will feel comfortable leading God's people in their new assignment.

Figure 15. Qualities of the bishop and church leader (Titus 5:6-9)

It is clear that the requirements for church leaders are many. But these many requirements are important for them to be a good example to everyone. The unsaved must see good qualities in church leaders and want to follow the same God that they serve.

It must be known that not all church leaders will be married or have children, and that both men and women can be appointed as church leaders. God is more interested in their ability to lead rather than their gender.

18. Appoint licensed and anointed leaders

The works of the Lord have become very important in many communities and countries. Those who are assigned to perform God's assignment may have to be licensed to do the work of the Lord.

It must be known that licensing leaders does not give them the power to do whatever they want to do. That is outside of biblical teachings. Being licensed is not what allows the Spirit of God to rest upon them.

Those who will be issued with a license must be trained and complete some studies, assignments, and practical works in Christian service. Sending novices to do the work of God will only cause damage to the body of Christ.

> **1 Timothy 3:5-7**
>
> 5 (For if a man know not how to rule his own house, how shall
> he take care of the church of God?) 6 Not a novice, lest being
> lifted up with pride he fall into the condemnation of the devil.
> 7 Moreover he must have a good report of them which are
> without; lest he fall into reproach and the snare of the devil.

Some churches will only appoint new leaders who have completed some formal biblical training. This may include, but is not limited to, attending Bible college. Besides attending Bible college or school, these leaders will need to be active members in their local church, including spending time learning in Bible studies.

It is important that new church leaders be given opportunities to practice their calling within the parent church. From the practice that they receive, they will become efficient in the assignment that is set before them at the new church.

Most congregations have many members who possess work experience and academic qualifications. They will expect their church leaders to be qualified in biblical teaching so as to guide them properly concerning the things of God and even in their social lives. Church leaders are called not only to be spiritual leaders but leaders in so many other important areas of human services.

18.1 Appoint Spirit-filled leaders

In the New Testament, God was moving mightily among his people. The leaders were much occupied with God's work, and some of them did not get to perform certain other important duties. Therefore, a call was made for other leaders to be appointed to perform other duties for God. This request was reasonable to the disciples, and they asked for seven men to be chosen. The following table shows the qualifications for these men who were to be appointed.

Table 6. Qualifying guidelines for the seven leaders in Acts 6:3

Criteria	Explanation
Men of honest report	The lifestyle of those chosen must be a good testimony to the body of Christ. The lives of these men had to be proven to be good before they were appointed to become leaders. If these men were wise but had bad reports among the people with whom they dwelt, then they would not meet the full requirements.
Full of the Holy Ghost	To do the works of the Lord effectively involves more than just head knowledge. Many intellectual persons who do not have the Holy Spirit cannot do the spiritual aspect of God's work. A person can have master's and first degrees, but if they lack the Holy Spirit, then they cannot do the spiritual things that God needs to be done for his people.
Wisdom	The kingdom of God cannot operate in ignorance. Therefore, those who are appointed to leadership

positions in the church must be wise, both in the things of God and in many aspects of social life.

Acts 6:1-7

1 And in those days, when the number of the disciples was multiplied, there arose a murmuring of the Grecians against the Hebrews, because their widows were neglected in the daily ministration. 2 Then the twelve called the multitude of the disciples unto them, and said, It is not reason that we should leave the word of God, and serve tables. 3 Wherefore, brethren, look ye out among you seven men of honest report, full of the Holy Ghost and wisdom, whom we may appoint over this business. 4 But we will give ourselves continually to prayer, and to the ministry of the word. 5 And the saying pleased the whole multitude: and they chose Stephen, a man full of faith and of the Holy Ghost, and Philip, and Prochorus, and Nicanor, and Timon, and Parmenas, and Nicolas a proselyte of Antioch: 6 Whom they set before the apostles: and when they had prayed, they laid their hands on them. 7 And the word of God increased; and the number of the disciples multiplied in Jerusalem greatly; and a great company of the priests were obedient to the faith.

18.2 People without God's Spirit cannot cast out demons

One of the things that many church leaders will have to do is to cast out demons. This may not be a regular activity for them, but they must be equipped to do it when necessary. Being equipped means that they need the Holy Spirit to cast out the evil spirit.

The sons of Sceva thought that casting out demons was an ordinary thing and that they could have done it too. Well, they learned a lesson, which caused them much public embarrassment. The lesson is simple: leave the spiritual things to those who have God's Spirit upon them.

Acts 19:13-18

13 Then certain of the vagabond Jews, exorcists, took upon
them to call over them which had evil spirits the name of
the LORD Jesus, saying, We adjure you by Jesus whom Paul
preacheth. 14 And there were seven sons of one Sceva, a Jew,
and chief of the priests, which did so. 15 And the evil spirit
answered and said, Jesus I know, and Paul I know; but who are
ye? 16 And the man in whom the evil spirit was leaped on them,
and overcame them, and prevailed against them, so that they
fled out of that house naked and wounded. 17 And this was
known to all the Jews and Greeks also dwelling at Ephesus;
and fear fell on them all, and the name of the Lord Jesus was
magnified. 18 And many that believed came, and confessed, and
shewed their deeds.

18.3 Endowed with God's Spirit

Leaders who will be assigned to new churches must also seek God for his Spirit to fill their lives. They must be aware that they are going on a great assignment in which they do not know many of the things that will happen to them, but the Holy Spirit will guide them. It may take some time to wait on God's Spirit, but it is a worthwhile wait.

Acts 1:3-8

3 To whom also he shewed himself alive after his passion by
many infallible proofs, being seen of them forty days, and
speaking of the things pertaining to the kingdom of God:
4 And, being assembled together with them, commanded them
that they should not depart from Jerusalem, but wait for the
promise of the Father, which, saith he, ye have heard of me.
5 For John truly baptized with water; but ye shall be baptized
with the Holy Ghost not many days hence. 6 When they
therefore were come together, they asked of him, saying, Lord,
wilt thou at this time restore again the kingdom to Israel? 7 And
he said unto them, It is not for you to know the times or the
seasons, which the Father hath put in his own power. 8 But ye
shall receive power, after that the Holy Ghost is come upon

> you: and ye shall be witnesses unto me both in Jerusalem, and in all Judaea, and in Samaria, and unto the uttermost part of the earth.

Jesus asked the believers to wait for the Holy Spirit (Acts 1:3-8, 2:1-5). Whatever the Lord promised, he will deliver. He just wants his people to wait for him. He knew that the Holy Spirit was needed for the believers to be effective in their ministries.

Acts 2:1-5

> [1] And when the day of Pentecost was fully come, they were all
> with one accord in one place. [2] And suddenly there came a
> sound from heaven as of a rushing mighty wind, and it filled
> all the house where they were sitting. [3] And there appeared
> unto them cloven tongues like as of fire, and it sat upon each
> of them. [4] And they were all filled with the Holy Ghost, and
> began to speak with other tongues, as the Spirit gave them
> utterance. [5] And there were dwelling at Jerusalem Jews, devout
> men, out of every nation under heaven.

18.4 Apostle Paul encouraged believers to receive the Holy Spirit

The Apostle Paul, having been saved by the Lord, started to work for the Lord. He chose to serve the Lord who saved him, and he was zealous in sharing God's good news with others. He moved from village to village preaching about the kingdom of God (Acts 19:1). As a leader, he was not ashamed of the gospel of Jesus Christ but bold in proclaiming the Lord wherever he went (Acts 19:8-10).

Apostle Paul did not only teach about God's kingdom but also encouraged believers to receive the Holy Spirit (Acts 19:2-6). He baptized them in the name of Jesus and with the Holy Spirit. These leaders now had the Holy Spirit in their lives to work for God.

Acts 19:1-12

> [1] And it came to pass, that, while Apollos was at Corinth, Paul
> having passed through the upper coasts came to Ephesus: and
> finding certain disciples, [2] He said unto them, Have ye received

> the Holy Ghost since ye believed? And they said unto him, We have not so much as heard whether there be any Holy Ghost. 3 And he said unto them, Unto what then were ye baptized? And they said, Unto John's baptism. 4 Then said Paul, John verily baptized with the baptism of repentance, saying unto the people, that they should believe on him which should come after him, that is, on Christ Jesus. 5 When they heard this, they were baptized in the name of the Lord Jesus. 6 And when Paul had laid his hands upon them, the Holy Ghost came on them; and they spake with tongues, and prophesied. 7 And all the men were about twelve.
>
> 8 And he went into the synagogue, and spake boldly for the space of three months, disputing and persuading the things concerning the kingdom of God. 9 But when divers were hardened, and believed not, but spake evil of that way before the multitude, he departed from them, and separated the disciples, disputing daily in the school of one Tyrannus. 10 And this continued by the space of two years; so that all they which dwelt in Asia heard the word of the Lord Jesus, both Jews and Greeks. 11 And God wrought special miracles by the hands of Paul: 12 So that from his body were brought unto the sick handkerchiefs or aprons, and the diseases departed from them, and the evil spirits went out of them.

All believers are expected to seek God for his Spirit. It is a free gift from God, which will make the works of the Lord easy for all believers. Persons who are assigned to new churches must also carry the Holy Spirit with them, so that God can fill the house, perform miracles, and bless the lives of the congregants.

19. Farewell service for new appointees

When persons are assigned to continue the work of the Lord at the new church, there must be a farewell service, and it must be well coordinated.

Some churches quietly send off new leaders to do the work of the Lord at the new church. However, that must change, since those who are assigned to the new church have labored at the existing church, and their efforts and contributions must be acknowledged.

19.1 Honor those who labored

The farewell service is an important sending-off of God's people to new assignments. Those who are assigned to the new church must know that their fellow workers in God's kingdom appreciate what they have done over the years at the current church and that they have been given a new assignment to continue the work of the Lord at another location.

> **Romans 13:7-8**
>
> [7] Render therefore to all their dues: tribute to whom tribute is due; custom to whom custom; fear to whom fear; honour to whom honour. [8] Owe no man anything, but to love one another: for he that loveth another hath fulfilled the law.
>
> **1 Peter 2:17**
>
> [17] Honour all men. Love the brotherhood. Fear God. Honour the king.

Romans 12:10

[10] Be kindly affectioned one to another with brotherly love; in honour preferring one another.

Proverbs 3:27

[27] Withhold not good from them to whom it is due, when it is in the power of thine hand to do it.

19.2 Planned farewell service

The farewell service must not be seen as an ordinary service. Much effort must be given to this service, as it must be planned in advance and be well executed.

Family members of those who will be sent to the new church must be invited to this important service. Seating arrangements must be adequate and reserved for family members and special invitees.

Ushers must be assigned to ensure that when the members who will be sent off are ready to enter the church for the farewell service, they are well greeted and taken to their seats. They must be treated like royalty, as they are great persons in the kingdom of God who are about to embark on another important journey for the Lord, but at a new location.

If it is possible, testimonies can be shared at the farewell service from persons who know and have worked with them. It would be sad to see that no one has anything good to share about those who will be assigned to the new church.

Meals or snacks must be prepared and shared at the farewell service. If food cannot be provided for everyone, there must at least be snacks and meals for those who are assigned to the new church.

19.3 Honor the entire family and all assignees

Sometimes, too much emphasis is placed on one person who will be assigned to the new church. For example, persons may spend too much time talking about the pastor who will be assigned to the new church. If that leader has a family, then their entire family must be acknowledged throughout the farewell service.

If other members of the church have also been assigned to the new church, then they must also be acknowledged in the farewell service. When too much attention is focused on one individual, it can create unease in the minds of the other persons who are assigned to the new church.

19.4 Give new assignees an opportunity to speak before their departure

Depending upon the number of persons who have been assigned to the new church and will be at the farewell service, some or all of them should be given an opportunity to give their departing speech. They must be told in advance that their speech will be brief since there are other persons who will be speaking as well.

Members often feel encouraged when they are treated great. In return, they will practice the same thing when they have to release other members to new assignments for the Lord.

19.5 Brief preaching

A guide and reminder to church leaders: please let your preaching and teaching at the farewell service be strategic and brief. Remember that there are other important things to be done at the farewell service.

Much of the attention at this service must be on encouraging the new assignees. At this service, the congregants must be reminded of the church's mission and that everyone must be involved in winning souls and continuing the work of the Lord. After listening to the sermon, other members must feel stirred to become involved in church planting and understand that God wants to meet the needs of everyone.

19.6 Anointing new church leaders and other assignees

Anointing the new church leaders and those who will be assigned to labor with them in God's vineyard is of great importance. The works that have to be done for the Lord cannot be completed with human strength alone.

Zechariah 4:6

> [6] Then he answered and spake unto me, saying, this is the word of the LORD unto Zerubbabel, saying, Not by might, nor by power, but by my spirit, saith the LORD of hosts.

The anointing of the new church leaders and other assignees can be done at the farewell service or at another service beforehand. It is important to send them all off with the presence and blessings of God. They are embarking on a great mission and need spiritual strength to execute God's assignment.

God wanted to ease the work that Moses was doing, so he commanded Moses to gather seventy men of the Elders of Israel so that he could place his Spirit upon them and work through them. This must have been a welcome relief to Moses, who had much to do for the Lord.

Numbers 11:16-17

> [16] And the LORD said unto Moses, Gather unto me seventy men of the elders of Israel, whom thou knowest to be the elders of the people, and officers over them; and bring them unto the tabernacle of the congregation, that they may stand there with thee. [17] And I will come down and talk with thee there: and I will take of the spirit which is upon thee, and will put it upon them; and they shall bear the burden of the people with thee, that thou bear it not thyself alone.

It is expected that many modern-day church leaders will work with God to appoint other leaders to do the works of the Lord. These new leaders need the Spirit of God to execute the Lord's assignment.

After God told the prophet Samuel to anoint David as the next king, then Samuel anointed David for this important office. It is important that when the people of God are called to certain offices and ministries, they are anointed for those positions.

1 Samuel 16:11-13

[11] And Samuel said unto Jesse, Are here all thy children? And he said, There remaineth yet the youngest, and, behold, he keepeth the sheep. And Samuel said unto Jesse, Send and fetch him: for we will not sit down till he come hither. [12] And he sent, and brought him in. Now he was ruddy, and withal of a beautiful countenance, and goodly to look to. And the LORD said, Arise, anoint him: for this is he. [13] Then Samuel took the horn of oil, and anointed him in the midst of his brethren: and the Spirit of the LORD came upon David from that day forward. So Samuel rose up, and went to Ramah.

The anointing of church leaders and other members can be done as a private sermon, and it can also be done in the presence of others. What is most important is that those who will be taking up new appointments must be anointed for the works that are set before them.

19.7 Appointment letter

The works of the Lord must be professionally executed. The senior leader at the parent church, district overseers, General Overseer, or an authorized high-ranking official within the denomination must issue appointment letters to those members who are assigned to the new church.

This letter must give clear guidance, especially to the new church leaders, of what their expectations are. While the letter cannot capture everything, it must work as a guide for the new leaders to know what they are asked to do for the Lord.

The other persons who will be assigned to the new church must also be issued with letters notifying them of their new responsibilities and thanking them for their service. People often feel appreciated when they are treated with respect, and that may prompt them to want to do more.

The appointment letter cannot dictate how the Spirit of God will operate in the services at the new church. However, it is expected that the new leaders will invite and encourage the Holy Spirit to always be a part of their services and to lead the people of God.

Some church leaders may call the appointment letter an assignment letter. Whatever name is used, the essence of the letter is to provide a formal document indicating what the new leaders are broadly expected to do for God and thanking them for taking on the responsibility to work for God at a new physical location.

The appointment letter must be prepared on the church's letterhead or stamped with the church's stamp. The appointment letters for all new assignees must be in envelopes with their names written on them.

Thank-you cards can also be given to the new assignees. However, the thank-you card is not the same as an appointment letter and must not be used as a replacement for appointment letters. Therefore, it is essential to provide appointment letters to all new assignees.

19.8 Monetary donations

For some churches, a special offering will be collected from the congregation at the parent church and given to the leaders of the new church. This is another good thing for them to do to assist the new church financially with the works of the Lord, but it is not a requirement.

20. The opening ceremony for new churches

Some church leaders would prefer to make the opening ceremony a small thing, because they like to be quiet in the things that they are doing for the Lord.

However, they must seek to gain maximum publicity from this opening ceremony. They must be willing to boast about their God. They must let the world know that it is God who has caused them to establish this new church so that lives will be saved and people will receive instructions from the Lord.

> **Psalm 34:1-3**
>
> [1] I will bless the LORD at all times: his praise shall continually be in my mouth. [2] My soul shall make her boast in the LORD: the humble shall hear thereof, and be glad. [3] O magnify the LORD with me, and let us exalt his name together.

20.1 Invite many dignitaries to the opening ceremony

Make the opening ceremony a grand event and invite many dignitaries. Let them know that something great has happened, and that they are invited to celebrate this great event.

When dignitaries are invited, some of them may want to join the church membership because of what they see the Lord is doing through that church. There are many dignitaries who need salvation, so it may be an ideal opportunity for them to know the Lord as their personal Savior. These are some important persons for consideration to be invited to the opening ceremony:

- President of the country
- Prime minister

- Ministers of government (including the ministers of education, culture, finance, etc.)
- Leaders of the opposition parties
- Commissioner of police
- Judges and magistrates
- Mayors
- Business owners
- Religious leaders from other denominations
- Media house representatives

These are only some of the important persons who must be considered as invited guests. These are influential persons, and their presence can cause many persons to become aware of the church.

20.2 A special committee for the church opening ceremony

A special committee must be established to plan for the opening ceremony, since this will be a major event. Organizers must ensure that they review their plans regularly before the final day and make any adjustments that will enable the event to be great.

Seating, lighting, washrooms, and parking are some things that are expected to be well coordinated. If snacks are shared, then that must be properly organized as well.

There will be a need for official invitations to be issued. That must be done early, and follow-up calls should be made to ensure that the invitees will be attending. Once some dignitaries have indicated that they will attend, then appropriate parking and seating arrangements must be put in place.

At the opening ceremony, efforts must be made for this service to be recorded. Persons can also decide to live stream it so as to gain more publicity and to include those who will not be able to attend the physical service.

Not all dignitaries will be able to spend at the event. Therefore, decide who those invited speakers will be.

20.3 Time management and receiving an offering at the opening ceremony

The opening ceremony must not be a very long service. It is important to have good time management and good use of resources. Persons who will be participating must practice whatever they have to do, so that on the day of the ceremony, they will give their best service.

For some opening ceremonies, it may be appropriate to receive an offering from all those in attendance. There is no need to compel anyone to give, but let them give of their own free will.

Information about the church, such as the time of services, its address, its telephone number, and its email address, must be provided to the invitees. This allows many persons to become aware of the church and when its services are held. Remember that the opening ceremony is a good time to market the church and promote the kingdom of God.

If persons have made financial and other contributions to the construction of the church, then their names can be mentioned. It may not be possible to name all of the financial contributors, so decide if any of their names should be mentioned, and if so, then be selective in whose names to include. Make the opening ceremony a memorable one.

20.4 Let God's presence fill the church

Most of all, let God's presence be felt in the sanctuary. It is important not to be too occupied with all the human celebrations but to let the Lord be praised. God likes when his children make his name great during anything that they have to do. He often will make his presence felt.

King Solomon had the opportunity to dedicate the temple that he had constructed. He spared nothing in making this a great event. He allowed the musicians to give praise to God. The place was so rich with the presence of God that even the servants of God could not stand in the temple because the Lord was there to make his presence felt (2 Chronicles 5:12-14). This was an awesome dedication service that King Solomon had. Today, many church leaders must also work toward having such a great time in the presence of the Lord that many of the invitees will have an encounter with the presence of the almighty God and want to attend the church's other services.

2 Chronicles 5:1-14

1 Thus all the work that Solomon made for the house of the LORD was finished: and Solomon brought in all the things that David his father had dedicated; and the silver, and the gold, and all the instruments, put he among the treasures of the house of God. 2 Then Solomon assembled the elders of Israel, and all the heads of the tribes, the chief of the fathers of the children of Israel, unto Jerusalem, to bring up the ark of the covenant of the LORD out of the city of David, which is Zion. 3 Wherefore all the men of Israel assembled themselves unto the king in the feast which was in the seventh month. 4 And all the elders of Israel came; and the Levites took up the ark. 5 And they brought up the ark, and the tabernacle of the congregation, and all the holy vessels that were in the tabernacle, these did the priests and the Levites bring up. 6 Also king Solomon, and all the congregation of Israel that were assembled unto him before the ark, sacrificed sheep and oxen, which could not be told nor numbered for multitude. 7 And the priests brought in the ark of the covenant of the LORD unto his place, to the oracle of the house, into the most holy place, even under the wings of the cherubims: 8 For the cherubims spread forth their wings over the place of the ark, and the cherubims covered the ark and the staves thereof above. 9 And they drew out the staves of the ark, that the ends of the staves were seen from the ark before the oracle; but they were not seen without. And there it is unto this day.

10 There was nothing in the ark save the two tables which Moses put therein at Horeb, when the LORD made a covenant with the children of Israel, when they came out of Egypt. 11 And it came to pass, when the priests were come out of the holy place: (for all the priests that were present were sanctified, and did not then wait by course: 12 Also the Levites which were the

singers, all of them of Asaph, of Heman, of Jeduthun, with their sons and their brethren, being arrayed in white linen, having cymbals and psalteries and harps, stood at the east end of the altar, and with them an hundred and twenty priests sounding with trumpets:)
13 It came even to pass, as the trumpeters and singers were as one, to make one sound to be heard in praising and thanking the LORD; and when they lifted up their voice with the trumpets and cymbals and instruments of musick, and praised the LORD, saying, For he is good; for his mercy endureth for ever: that then the house was filled with a cloud, even the house of the LORD;
14 So that the priests could not stand to minister by reason of the cloud: for the glory of the LORD had filled the house of God.

20.5 Allow God to manifest himself in the dedication service

Not only did King Solomon plan the event well, but because of what he had done, God manifested his presence during the dedication service. Solomon, the leader, was involved in the service, and he chose to pray unto his God. His prayer was not a prayer of enticing words that he wanted to recite, but he prayed from his heart.

King Solomon was prepared to make this dedication service a great one (1 Chronicles 7:1). He had many animals available to be sacrificed (1 Chronicles 7:5). What Solomon did was pleasing to the Lord, and the Lord made his presence felt. The Lord caused fire to come down and consume the sacrifice (2 Chronicles 7:1).

2 Chronicles 7:1-11

1 Now when Solomon had made an end of praying, the fire came down from heaven, and consumed the burnt offering and the sacrifices; and the glory of the LORD filled the house.
2 And the priests could not enter into the house of the LORD, because the glory of the LORD had filled the LORD's house.
3 And when all the children of Israel saw how the fire came down, and the glory of the LORD upon the house, they bowed themselves with their faces to the ground upon the pavement, and worshipped, and praised the LORD, saying, For he is good;

for his mercy endureth for ever. 4 Then the king and all the
people offered sacrifices before the LORD. 5 And king
Solomon offered a sacrifice of twenty and two thousand oxen,
and an hundred and twenty thousand sheep: so the king and
all the people dedicated the house of God. 6 And the priests
waited on their offices: the Levites also with instruments of
musick of the LORD, which David the king had made to praise
the LORD, because his mercy endureth for ever, when David
praised by their ministry; and the priests sounded trumpets
before them, and all Israel stood.

7 Moreover Solomon hallowed the middle of the court that was
before the house of the LORD: for there he offered burnt
offerings, and the fat of the peace offerings, because the brasen
altar which Solomon had made was not able to receive the
burnt offerings, and the meat offerings, and the fat. 8 Also at
the same time Solomon kept the feast seven days, and all Israel
with him, a very great congregation, from the entering in of
Hamath unto the river of Egypt. 9 And in the eighth day they
made a solemn assembly: for they kept the dedication of the
altar seven days, and the feast seven days. 10 And on the three
and twentieth day of the seventh month he sent the people
away into their tents, glad and merry in heart for the goodness
that the LORD had shewed unto David, and to Solomon, and
to Israel his people. 11 Thus Solomon finished the house of
the LORD, and the king's house: and all that came into
Solomon's heart to make in the house of the LORD, and in his
own house, he prosperously effected.

King Solomon's dedication of the temple was not an ordinary dedication. He was not just going through the routine to say that he was dedicating the temple. King Solomon wanted to make a great impression to God about how important the dedication was to him.

God was so well pleased by the dedication service that he also spoke to Solomon at night (2 Chronicles 7:12-22). No believers must withhold praise and prayer from their God.

2 Chronicles 7:12-22

12 And the LORD appeared to Solomon by night, and said unto him, I have heard thy prayer, and have chosen this place to myself for an house of sacrifice. 13 If I shut up heaven that there be no rain, or if I command the locusts to devour the land, or if I send pestilence among my people; 14 If my people, which are called by my name, shall humble themselves, and pray, and seek my face, and turn from their wicked ways; then will I hear from heaven, and will forgive their sin, and will heal their land. 15 Now mine eyes shall be open, and mine ears attent unto the prayer that is made in this place. 16 For now have I chosen and sanctified this house, that my name may be there for ever: and mine eyes and mine heart shall be there perpetually.

17 And as for thee, if thou wilt walk before me, as David thy father walked, and do according to all that I have commanded thee, and shalt observe my statutes and my judgments; 18 Then will I stablish the throne of thy kingdom, according as I have covenanted with David thy father, saying, There shall not fail thee a man to be ruler in Israel. 19 But if ye turn away, and forsake my statutes and my commandments, which I have set before you, and shall go and serve other gods, and worship them; 20 Then will I pluck them up by the roots out of my land which I have given them; and this house, which I have sanctified for my name, will I cast out of my sight, and will make it to be a proverb and a byword among all nations. 21 And this house, which is high, shall be an astonishment to every one that passeth by it; so that he shall say, Why hath the LORD done thus unto this land, and unto this house? 22 And it shall be answered, Because they forsook the LORD God of their fathers, which brought them forth out of the land of Egypt, and laid hold on other gods, and worshipped them, and served them: therefore hath he brought all this evil upon them.

Every church dedication service must be done with the primary intention of honoring God. The participation of everyone must be coordinated, and the focus of their praise must not be for the glory of man but for the Lord almighty.

20.6 Anniversary church services

Church leaders must not stop at the opening service; they must continue to have anniversary services each year. Through these annual services, many persons will get to know the church and the Lord. The opening and anniversary services must also be used as a soul-winning approach. At these services, many persons may be attending a church after a long time or for the first time. During some of these services, an entire family may be saved and added to the church.

21. Develop sustainable networks

Every church leader must seek to develop a network with many persons and organizations. These networks must not be because the church leaders want something from them, but in order to present the church as an important organization within the community.

For example, leaders may organize feeding programs. These leaders will be involved in feeding schoolchildren, elderly persons in the community, or disabled persons.

These are some organizations that the church and its leaders can develop relationships with. Many of these organizations know about the importance of the church.

- Learning institutions
- Hospitals and health centers
- Law enforcement organizations
- Supermarkets
- Taxi services
- Government and private-sector organizations
- Utility companies

The list above is not exhaustive, but these are some important organizations that can be found in every community.

While churches may belong to different denominations, they are serving the same Lord. In some communities, church leaders will network to host crusades and prayer meetings.

Proverbs 17:17

[17]A friend loveth at all times, and a brother is born for adversity.

Colossians 3:12-13

[12]Put on therefore, as the elect of God, holy and beloved, bowels of mercies, kindness, humbleness of mind, meekness, longsuffering; [13]Forbearing one another, and forgiving one another, if any man have a quarrel against any: even as Christ forgave you, so also do ye.

Job 6:14

[14]To him that is afflicted pity should be shewed from his friend; but he forsaketh the fear of the Almighty.

Proverbs 27:9

[9]Ointment and perfume rejoice the heart: so doth the sweetness of a man's friend by hearty counsel.

God wants his children to live in unity. The children of God must be a good reflection of God on the earth as they build sustainable networks with others.

22. Attracting new members to new churches

The church leaders must be on a mission to attract new members to the church. The parent church may have a large congregation, but the new church leaders will have to build their own membership. This increase in membership may not occur in only a few days, so there is work to be done to grow the membership for the new church.

Figure 16. Approaches in attracting new members to churches

Crusades and revival services
Organize for healing and deliverance services
Allow the Holy Spirit to be at work in each service
Constantly teach God's Word and use practical examples
Utilize great ushers and greeters
Children's ministry, Sunday school, and daycare
Establish a cafeteria
Concerts and cultural events
Visitation and sharing of tracts
Community outreach
Participate in learning institutions' activities
Lifestyle of the church members and the leaders
Active and interactive social media platforms
Hosting friends and family days
Invite family and friends to baptism
Use funeral services and weddings to promote the church
Honor persons in the community for their accomplishments
Develop a friendly personality
Direct and mass marketing
Active public relationships from the church

22.1 Crusades and revival services

Crusades and revival services are still impactful in attracting persons to churches. Many persons will attend these services to be touched by the hands of God. They may eventually become members of the church because of what the Lord has done for them. Crusades and revival services are services that often provide opportunities for persons to accept Jesus Christ as their Lord and Savior. Once they accept him, then they have salvation.

22.2 Organize for healing and deliverance services

People are sick, and they need the healing hands of God to touch them and cause them to be made whole. Peter and John were entering the house of God to pray, and there was a man who was begging. While they did not offer him money, they prayed for him, and he was made whole. He went into the temple, leaping and praising God, because he was excited about his healing.

> **Acts 3:1-10**
>
> 1 Now Peter and John went up together into the temple at the hour of prayer, being the ninth hour. 2 And a certain man lame from his mother's womb was carried, whom they laid daily at the gate of the temple which is called Beautiful, to ask alms of them that entered into the temple; 3 Who seeing Peter and John about to go into the temple asked an alms. 4 And Peter, fastening his eyes upon him with John, said, Look on us. 5 And he gave heed unto them, expecting to receive something of them.
>
> 6 Then Peter said, Silver and gold have I none; but such as I have give I thee: In the name of Jesus Christ of Nazareth rise up and walk. 7 And he took him by the right hand, and lifted him up: and immediately his feet and ankle bones received strength. 8 And he leaping up stood, and walked, and entered with them into the temple, walking, and leaping, and praising God. 9 And all the people saw him walking and praising God: 10 And they knew that it was he which sat for alms at the Beautiful gate of the temple: and they were filled with wonder and amazement at that which had happened unto him.

People often approached Jesus because they wanted him to heal them, and he did so on many occasions. So, if the church is able to offer healing and deliverance services, then they can expect that many persons will join the church.

22.3 Allow the Holy Spirit to be at work in each service

People will be added to the church when the Holy Spirit is at work. Believers need to allow God's Spirit to constantly flow through all of their services, and more persons will be added to the church.

> **Acts 2:42-47**
>
> [42] And they continued stedfastly in the apostles' doctrine and
> fellowship, and in breaking of bread, and in prayers. [43] And fear
> came upon every soul: and many wonders and signs were done
> by the apostles. [44] And all that believed were together, and had
> all things common; [45] And sold their possessions and goods,
> and parted them to all men, as every man had need. [46] And they,
> continuing daily with one accord in the temple, and breaking
> bread from house to house, did eat their meat with gladness
> and singleness of heart, [47] Praising God, and having favour with
> all the people. And the Lord added to the church daily such as
> should be saved.

As the Apostles continued to teach and exhort the people, God added to the church daily (Acts 2:47). This became possible because the Holy Spirit was at work during the sessions that the Apostles had with the people.

22.4 Constantly teach God's Word and use practical examples

As believers, no one has to manufacture the Good News, as it is already there in the Bible. Believers are required to teach the Good News, and when they do, people will be drawn to the kingdom. The Good News must be presented in a simple way, probably along with practical examples, and people will be drawn to the kingdom. If the Good News is taught and preached using complex information, many persons may take a very long time to understand what is in the Good News for them. Additionally, the practical examples used by church leaders during their teaching and preaching services must not be immoral or offensive.

As Jesus taught the people, he used parables and other examples that they could easily connect with. His preaching never deviated from the truth.

Matthew 22:36-40

36 Master, which is the great commandment in the law? 37 Jesus said unto him, Thou shalt love the Lord thy God with all thy heart, and with all thy soul, and with all thy mind. 38 This is the first and great commandment. 39 And the second is like unto it, Thou shalt love thy neighbour as thyself. 40 On these two commandments hang all the law and the prophets.

Utilize great ushers and greeters

Church leaders must have their ushers and greeters trained to deliver exceptional service to everyone who attends the house of God. Good ushers will allow persons to feel at home whenever they visit the church. Poor ushering will cause persons to hate the church and its members. Ushers and greeters must have a pleasant personality, be willing to smile, and carefully direct persons to their seats. The lifestyle of ushers and greeters outside of church must be consistent with Bible teachings.

22.5 Children's ministry, Sunday school, and daycare

Many persons in the community may be looking for a religious place to send their children to hear the word of God. Therefore, offering children's church and Sunday schools may also cause many parents and other adults to join the church.

If there is enough land space and funds, the church can establish a daycare. It will need to be in keeping with the zoning of the area and other regulations for that community. However, if it is possible to establish a daycare, many adults may soon become connected to the church, since they know where to find it and their children may be involved in church activities.

22.6 Establish a cafeteria

Whether young or old, everyone has the need for food. Therefore, if the church can offer meals at affordable prices, then it may cause more persons to visit the church. During weekly church services, the cafeteria can be made available to persons who want to purchase meals and beverages. The quality of the meals and services must allow persons to constantly be satisfied in how they are spending their money.

22.7 Concerts and cultural events

Many persons like to attend church concerts and cultural events. They have the opportunity to hear great singing and see many persons involved in such events. Drama, dancing, and poetry may be captivating to many persons. These events often have a way of causing visitors to like the church, and they may soon decide to become members because they recognize that their spiritual needs are met at the church.

22.8 Visitation and sharing of tracts

The members of the church must also be involved in church visitations. This is another direct and practical way of attracting persons to the church. When members visit persons in the community or surrounding communities, they can leave with them some tracts and other information about the church and where it is located. The time spent with each person during the time of visitation does not have to be lengthy, but it must be impactful.

22.9 Community outreach

Community outreach activities are good ways for members of the church to demonstrate that they care about the community. This may include clean-up exercises or repainting an important building. Church members might help the elderly in the community to get some fresh air and allow them to walk in the park. There are many persons in communities who want to see and hear from the church members. Those members who are involved in community outreach should wear clothes that identify the church's name, or they should have some form of identification so that persons know which church they are connected to. Many organizations are involved in branding and community outreach, and churches can adopt a similar approach of getting people to know about the church and where it is located.

22.10 Participate in learning institutions' activities

Some learning institutions may need a member of the church to participate in the opening prayer when the school reopens for the new academic year. If the learning institution has a cultural event, then they may need an item from the church, so this will be a good opportunity for the church to participate in such an important activity.

Sometimes, members of the church are also students, so they can promote their church at their learning institutions. Those members can also seek to find out how their church leadership can be more actively involved in activities at the learning institution. For example, bembers of the church can be involved in leading a Bible club or teaching moral education at these learning institutions.

There are so many ways for the church to participate in learning institutions. Some of the teachers and lecturers may be believers, and they may be looking for opportunities for other believers to partner with them to do the works of the Lord.

22.11 Lifestyle of the church members and the leaders

The lifestyle of church members can either attract persons to churches or distract them from attending. Therefore, every church member must remember that they are ambassadors for the kingdom of God, and therefore, their lifestyle must be consistent with the Bible.

> **Matthew 5:13-16**
>
> 13 Ye are the salt of the earth: but if the salt have lost his savour,
> wherewith shall it be salted? it is thenceforth good for nothing,
> but to be cast out, and to be trodden under foot of men. 14 Ye
> are the light of the world. A city that is set on an hill cannot be
> hid. 15 Neither do men light a candle, and put it under a bushel,
> but on a candlestick; and it giveth light unto all that are in the

house. [16] Let your light so shine before men, that they may see your good works, and glorify your Father which is in heaven.

22.12 Active and interactive social media platforms

Many churches have at least one social media platform, and those that do not should begin to utilize at least one. If they have social media, they can promote things that are happening at the church. Some parts of the regular church services can also be posted on the social media platform.

The social media platform used by the church must allow persons to interact with the church by making comments or asking questions.

Regular updates about the church must be on the social media platform. Information about the church's location, telephone number, and service times must also be available for persons who will use that option to communicate with the church. A professional and reliable person must be assigned to monitor this communication and provide responses from the church.

22.13 Hosting friends and family days

The church must be an active organization in society that attracts sinners and saints and gives them an opportunity to feel love and appreciated. Persons must know that the Lord hates their sins, but he does not hate them. He wants them to come to him, and he will heal and deliver them. If people feel that the church is a place where sinners cannot attend, then they will remain sinners because they do not have any hope that Christ died for their sins and wants to save them.

For friends and family days, persons can be involved in doing things that they are better at, which will be consistent with God's teaching. It may be important to provide some criteria and guidelines for the participation of persons in that service and for the activities that they would like to perform.

22.14 Invite family and friends to baptism

When the church has baptisms, friends and family must be invited. This must be seen as an important event for the person who has accepted the Lord as their personal Savior. Friends and family can also participate in singing religious songs on that day or taking photographs of the persons they have come to support. The involvement of friends and family in baptism may cause more persons to want to be baptized and join the church.

22.15 Use funeral services and weddings to promote the church

Many persons will attend churches for weddings and funerals. These are great opportunities for persons to get to know more about the church. The ushers can give the attendees written material that contains information about the church and its services. After weddings and funerals, persons may want a place to become their home church, and the information presented to them at the time of their visit may be enough to help them decide if they want to continue serving the Lord at that church.

22.16 Honor persons in the community for their accomplishments

In the community, there are many things that church members can be involved in—for example, honoring students who perform well in school, honoring great athletes in the community, and celebrating the birthday of senior citizens who have attained the age of 80, 90, 100, etc. Church members might honor school teachers on their retirement or celebrate law enforcement officers for anything outstanding that they have done recently. People must not only hear that a church is in their community, they must see the church being an active part of the community, and they must also feel the love of God through the church members.

22.17 Develop a friendly personality

Leaders of the church can spend some time teaching church members to develop friendly personalities. Besides the great movement of God in the services, persons want to know that they are in a friendly church where people care about them. When each church service is over, members must meet and greet visitors and friends. If a visitor or new member does not have their own transportation and lives in the same direction that a church member has to travel, then that member may be willing to take them to their destination.

22.18 Direct and mass marketing

The church always has good news to share. They must not be afraid to share the news of Jesus Christ and what the Lord is doing at the church. The leaders of the church can organize for paid advertisements about the church and its activities. Sometimes, church members can engage in direct communication with persons to inform them about the church. When church members attend learning institutions, schools, and supermarkets, they can tell persons about the Lord and where the church is located.

22.19 Active public relationships from the church

The leadership of the church can be involved in public relationships. They can constantly promote things that are happening at the church. If there is a concert and crusade, then such information ought to be made available. When the church is celebrating important anniversaries (5, 10, 15 years), then this important information ought to be shared with the public direction that a church member has to travel, then that member may be willing to pass them for their denomination.

2.7.8 Direct post mail marketing

[illegible]

[illegible]

[illegible]

23. Provide progress and praise reports

Leaders who are assigned to new churches must remember that they have to provide reports and feedback. There may be some standard reports or forms that they have to complete. They should not find this difficult, as everyone is accountable to someone.

Luke 10:17

17 And the seventy returned again with joy, saying, Lord, even the devils are subject unto us through thy name.

Not all denominations may require their leaders to provide reports. However, the following sample information will help some leaders with regular reporting.

23.1 Report on church growth

New church leaders may have to provide a report about church growth. This will include, the number of persons who gave their lives to the Lord, were baptized, or were transferred to the church from other churches. There will be situations where some members will seek a transfer to go to another church, and this will result in a reduction of the church membership.

Those who receive these reports must not just file the reports away but analyze them, as it can speak about the health of the church. There may not be regular movements in church growth every month, but it is expected that some of the numbers will change during the year. Leaders who are not attracting new members may have to be further assessed, as every leader must make attempts to win souls as often as possible.

23.2 Report on financial performance

The church's financial performance is the topic of another report that many leaders are expected to submit. This report may need to be submitted monthly. It may have a specific format and will show all sources of revenue that the church received for the reporting period.

Reporting about the church's finances may be important, especially if the church has to repay loans or mortgages. The leader of the church also needs to be earning sufficient income to provide for their family.

23.3 Report of community activities and outreach

Leaders should seek to be involved in community activities. Church leaders are expected to have crusades, Deeper Life sessions, training of persons in the community, etc. The church is there to meet more than the spiritual needs of the congregation. Some of the community activities that the church participates in will attract new members.

23.4 Report on deaths and weddings

As part of their reporting, some church leaders will have to report about deaths and weddings. While these are two things that will not occur every week, it is important to know this information, as it can help with future planning of church activities.

23.5 Rejoicing for new souls

While church leaders can provide a progress report, which may just be filed away, there is rejoicing in heaven for every soul that is won. Therefore, the leaders must constantly win souls for the Lord. With more churches being established, every effort must be made to win more souls.

> **Luke 15:7**
>
> 7 I say unto you, that likewise joy shall be in heaven over one sinner that repenteth, more than over ninety and nine just persons, which need no repentance.

Reference list

ACCA 2.1. (2000). *Information systems*. Foulks Lynch.

ACCA P5. (2010). *Advanced performance management*. BPP Publishing.

Cole, G. A. (1993). *Management theory and practice* (4th ed.). DP Publications.

Hughes, R., Ginnett, R. & Curphy, G. (2015). *Leadership: Enhancing the lessons of experience* (8th ed.). McGraw-Hill Education.

Lane, P. (1966). *Revision notes for Ordinary Level Economics*. Allman & Son Limited.

Noe, R. A., Hollenbeck, J. R., Gerhart, B., & Wright, P. M. (2015). *Human resource management: Gaining a competitive advantage* (9th ed.). McGraw-Hill Education.

PMI. (2008). *A guide to the Project Management Body of Knowledge (PMBOK)* (4th ed.). Project Management Institute.

Thompson, A., Peteraf, M., Gamble, J., & Strickland, A. J., III. (2014). *Crafting and executing strategy: The quest for competitive advantage: Concepts and cases* (19th ed.). McGraw-Hill Education.

Titman, S., Martin, T., Keown, A. J., & Martin, J. D. (2016). *Financial management: Principles and applications* (7th ed.). Pearson Australia.

About the author

Having been involved in evangelism for many years, Rev. Geary Reid has taught and preached to many persons. He knows that leaders want to increase their membership and create new churches. Therefore, he provides many practical ways of establishing new churches and attracting persons to a congregation.

Blessed with background knowledge in Project Management and Financial Management, he shares how leaders must see new churches as important projects. Leaders are challenged to consider all the costs associated with these projects. There are certain fixed and variable costs that must be included in the project budget. If the church leaders need to seek financing, they must know how much they will have to borrow.

Having been saved since 1986, Rev. Reid has experienced many things at many congregations as he goes to share God's word. Visiting many recently established churches, he has seen that there are areas in which some new leaders must improve. However, new leaders cannot always be blamed for their shortcomings, since some of them were not properly trained by the senior pastors who sent them out to lead new churches.

After listening to some of the challenges new church leaders are experiencing, Rev. Reid now provides solutions to many of those challenges. Some new leaders were assigned to new churches, but no appointment letters were issued to them. There are others who receive appointment letters that only provide limited information about what they are expected to do and what reports they have to complete on a regular basis.

Establishing new churches must be done in every denomination, as Jesus wants believers to take the gospel to everyone. Crusades will allow some persons to hear God's word for the first time, but those persons will then want to attend a permanent place to hear God's word regularly and to have fellowship with other believers. Establishing a new church involves much planning, so it must be done strategically. This planning must not be done by the senior leader of the church alone, but by a committee that is established to plan for new churches. As he has studied Strategic Management and has been involved in strategic planning on a regular basis, Geary Reid shares some practical ways in which church leaders can establish new churches.

Having been a leader in different ministries within the body of Christ, Reid wants leaders to be equipped for the assignment that is set before them. When new leaders are trained and equipped, they will cause their congregation to grow, and the Lord will bless their congregation. The Lord expects growth in every church, and he wants to see more churches being established to meet the needs of the people. Leaders, make it part of your church plan to strategically establish new churches.

www.ingramcontent.com/pod-product-compliance
Lightning Source LLC
LaVergne TN
LVHW052008160826
845678LV00005B/1679

* 9 7 8 9 7 6 8 3 0 5 7 4 9 *